AMAZING AND EXTRAORDINARY FACTS

THE
SCOTTISH
COUNTRYSIDE

AMAZING AND EXTRAORDINARY FACTS

THE
SCOTTISH COUNTRYSIDE

Ruth Binney

A Rydon Publishing Book
35 The Quadrant
Hassocks
West Sussex
BN6 8BP
www.rydonpublishing.co.uk
www.rydonpublishing.com

First published by Rydon Publishing in 2025

Copyright © Rydon Publishing 2025

Ruth Binney has asserted her right to be identified as author of this work in accordance with the Copyright, Designs and Patents Act, 1988.

All rights reserved. No part of this publication may be reproduced, stored in a retrieval system, or transmitted in any form or by any means, electronic or mechanical, by photocopying, recording or otherwise, without prior permission in writing from the publisher.

This book is sold subject to the condition that it shall not, by trade or otherwise, be lent, re-sold, hired out, or otherwise circulated without the publisher's prior consent in any form of binding or cover other than that in which it is published and without a similar condition including this condition being imposed on the subsequent purchaser.

The designs in this book are copyright and should not be made for resale.

A CIP catalogue record for this book is available from the British Library.

ISBN: 978-1-910821-43-5

Printed in the Czech Republic by FINIDR, s.r.o

CONTENTS

Introduction 8

THE WONDERS OF NATURE 10

MOODS OF THE HEAVENS 10
Rain and sun, mist and fog

THE GREATEST LIGHT SHOWS 13
Spectacular auroras – and other after dark effects

BELOW ZERO 15
The shapes and sounds of snow and ice

THE BITING CLOUDS 17
The scourge of the midge

AS WHITE AS SNOW 20
Keeping safe – and fed – in winter

LAPLAND COMES TO THE CAIRNGORMS 22
Scotland's reindeer herd

HISTORY IN THE ROCKS 24
Finding fossil treasures

ON TOP OF THE WORLD 26
Mighty mountains

WHERE EAGLES DARE 30
Magnificent raptors

TIMBER! 32
The world of pines

A FOREST REFUGE 36
Home for the elusive red squirrel

THE GREAT ACROBATS 38
Agile pine martens

ALL FOR SHOW 40
Mating rituals of the capercaillie and black grouse

MORE THAN JUST MUSHROOMS 42
Into the world of fungi

ON THE WING 46
Bats and butterflies, dragon and damselflies

HIDDEN WOODLAND GEMS 49
The extraordinary temperate rainforest

THE VALLEYS OF TIME *Glorious glens*	53	TUMBLING CASCADES *The wonders of waterfalls*	81
MONARCHS OF THE GLENS *Deer in their thousands*	57	SPIRITS OF THE WATER *The legendary kelpies*	83
AUTUMN ABUNDANCE *Berries of many kinds*	60	A TRIUMPH OF CONSERVATION *The osprey's successful return*	86
COMMON, CONTROVERSIAL AND ANCIENT *Flourishing ferns*	62	RARE AND RARER *Water wildlife, present and future*	87
SHADES OF PURPLE, PINK – AND LUCKY WHITE *All among the heather*	65	BESIDE STILL WATERS *Exploring freshwater lochs* DEEP, DARK AND MYSTERIOUS *The legendary Loch Ness*	89 93
GLORIOUS OR NOT? *The tale of the red grouse*	68	THE NESSIE MYSTERY *Monster of the loch*	95
REAL OR IMAGINARY? *Cats of the countryside*	71	NOT JUST NESSIE *Creatures of the lochs*	96
FOR PEAT'S SAKE *Precious carbon stores*	73	MASTERS OF THE WATER *The life of otters*	98
APPROACH WITH CAUTION *Plants with extraordinary powers*	77	LEAPING FOR THEIR LIVES *Salmon and their journeys*	100
THE HEIGHT OF BEAUTY *Scotland's alpine flora*	79		

USING THE LAND	**102**	THE ROMANS WERE HERE	125
A ROOF OVER YOUR HEAD	102	*The story of the Antonine Wall*	
Shelters past and present		TREASURE UNEARTHED	128
FOOD FOR THE NATION	104	*The countryside's hidden riches*	
All about oats		WARRIOR GHOSTS AND LASTING MEMORIALS	131
THE ESSENTIAL MALT	106	*The legacy of battle*	
Among the fields of barley		WHERE ART AND NATURE MEET	133
WHAT'S IN THAT FIELD?	108	*Sculpture in the landscape*	
Of crops and soil			
THE WONDERS OF WALLS	110		
Enclosing the landscape			
A WOOLLY TALE	112	**Index**	**136**
Scotland's special sheep		**Acknowledgements**	**144**
ICON OF THE HILLS	115		
The magnificent Heilan coo			
EXTRAORDINARY EQUINES	117		
Horses and their history			
RINGS OF STONE	120		
Witness to the ancient world			
MESSAGES IN THE STONES	123		
Cairns and their meanings			

INTRODUCTION

Everywhere, and in every season – and whatever the weather – Scotland's countryside is an endless source of wonder, enjoyment and discovery, whether on mountains or moorlands, in glens, woodlands and lochs, or in fields rich with traditional crops like oats and barley. In every landscape there is something special to admire, not least because Scotland is home to many animals and plants absent or rare in other parts of Britain, whether capercaille, pine martens and arctic hares, or wild raspberries, woolly willows and bleeding tooth fungi. And Scotland is home to the world's oldest known fossil, a single celled marine organism. Of all the extraordinary landscapes there are two that are in danger and deserving of particular care and attention – the ancient temperate rainforest of Argyll and the west Highlands, adorned with an incredible array of mosses, lichens and ferns, and the precious peatlands of the Flow Country, the 'black gold' of a warming world, which store 25 per cent more carbon than any other type of vegetation.

In so many ways, the countryside reflects a nation's history, both ancient and modern. Prehistoric faults and folds, and the forming and melting of ice, has shaped it dramatically, not least in the creation of the Great Glen the 400 million year old fault line that essentially separates Highlands and Lowlands, and the many U-shaped glens carved out as glaciers melted and retreated at the end of the last ice age, some 10,000 years ago. Even older are the many islands formed when a string of volcanoes collided with the mainland three billion years ago. In more recent times, the Highland Clearances of the 18th and 19th centuries in which many tenants of small farms were evicted, and their land replaced with large areas for sheep grazing, created great change. All over the countryside, from the magnificent Calanais Stones, megaliths on the Isle of Lewis, to remnants of the Antonine Wall built by Roman invaders and the Viking treasure of the Galloway Hoard, human history is everywhere to experience.

The countryside comes in every colour, from the white of fresh snow to the pinks and reds of heather and from the greens of pine forests to the deep black waters of Loch Ness. And its mood changes day by day, and from valley to mountain top. Such amazing variation has made the countryside an inspiration for generations of writers, poets and artists and, today, attracted film and programme makers who have made it the backdrop for productions from *Skyfall* and *Harry Potter* to *Call the Midwife*. There is mystery and magic here too. The hunt for Nessie goes on, and who knows when you might encounter a kelpie or Grampian giant. With popularity, however, comes the responsibility for all who visit and enjoy the countryside to treat it with utmost respect. There is a 'freedom to roam' in Scotland (with a few exceptions) which makes it even more important to care for the environment, be responsible for your own actions and leave no trace – save for a stone added to a mountaintop cairn.

On a personal note (and even despite the midges) I have loved Scotland's countryside since childhood, and with so much to explore on these pages have confined it to the areas away from the coast. I hope that they convey the magic and wonderment of a land beyond compare.

Ruth Binney
2025

THE WONDERS OF NATURE

The joy and beauty of the countryside lie in its natural assets, whether mountain wildernesses, carved by massive geological forces, the magnificent birds that roam its skies or the tiniest forest ferns. While many animals and plants are found in confined habitats, many are spread over huge areas, but the countryside's extraordinary natural world is grouped here largely by the wider ecosystems they create and inhabit. All are, of course, overlaid and enhanced by the weather and the seasons, making every day an amazing exploration.

MOODS OF THE HEAVENS
Rain and sun, mist and fog

It certainly rains, but not every day in Scotland is *dreich*, when heavy grey clouds scowl from above and, if it's not raining, could do so at any minute. Or it may be 'flenched' – promising to improve but never quite making it. And while the western Highlands are one of the wettest places in Europe, with an annual rainfall of around 4,500 mm (180 in) much of the east has about half that amount. Sunniest are the extreme eastern and southwestern coasts. On cold, clear nights, particularly in spring and autumn, clouds trap cold air close to the ground which turns to a clinging cloud (thick mist) as the water within condenses, a phenomenon called cloud inversion. From a hill or mountain top comes the experience of being above the clouds, surrounded by islands soaring from the mist.

EXTRAORDINARY FACT

IN THE CLOUDS

Clouds can come in extraordinary forms, especially in the Highlands. Lenticular clouds like flying saucers, sometimes with huge ridges and furrows within, appear over the peaks. Most dramatic at sunset, they form downwind of mountains where the land interrupts the airflow. Rare nacreous or 'mother of pearl' clouds, in shades of iridescent pastel colours most visible at sunrise and sunset, are created when very cold polar winds come south. At 15 to 20 km (9 to 12 miles) above the earth they are among the planet's highest. Horseshoe clouds, formed in vortices of rotating air, and rarities beloved of cloud watchers, last mere minutes.

QUICK FACTS

- Scotland is Europe's windiest country, thanks to its exposure to Atlantic depressions arriving from the west. A strong gust of wind is a *blenter*, *blouter*, *tiff* or *whidder*.

- Fine drizzle is known as *smirr*; thick drizzle is *dag*; dense drizzle is *smue*.

- Lightning strikes can shape the mountains by literally breaking rocks.

- In bright sunlight fogbows, much broader than rainbows, will form in thin mist.

THE BIG GREY MAN

On Ben Macdui in the Cairngorms, and at Lurchers Crag, the Big Grey Man (in Gaelic **Am Fear Liath Mòr***) or 'devil illusion' lives on. His presence is said to feel as if someone is walking behind you in the mist, every step crunching in the snow. Most likely this is the Brocken Spectre, a meteorological phenomenon that happens only when gaps in low cloud allow. When the sun is shining from behind you, you see a massive grey shadow of yourself stretching from your feet up into the cloud above. As the cloud moves, so the 'ghost' can seem to be walking. Even more spooky is the halo of rainbow coloured light that can appear around the shadow's head. The phenomenon is named from a peak in Germany's Harz mountains and described in 1780 by a pastor and natural historian Johann Silberschlag (1721-91).*

Brocken Spectre

THE GREATEST LIGHT SHOWS
Spectacular auroras – and other after dark effects

The night sky lit in dancing, swirling streams of green, pink, blue and purple is a magical sight. The wonders of the aurora borealis, the northern lights, are most prevalent in the far north and at the spring and autumn equinoxes when the earth's magnetic field is most closely aligned with that of the sun. Auroras arise when solar wind – streams of charged particles ejected from solar storms – disrupt the magnetosphere, the magnetic shield around our planet. As they do so they whip up huge waves, up to 15,000 km (9,320 miles) high and 40,000 km (25,000 miles) long which, as they break up, trigger geomagnetic storms setting off auroras. The variations in colour come from different gases – green from oxygen,

QUICK FACTS

- Aurora borealis means 'morning light coming from the north'.

- In Shetland the lights are called the Mirrie Dancers – *mirr* means 'to shimmer'.

- When light refracts from ice crystals it can form tall light pillars in the sky.

AMAZING FACT

ALL IN GREEN
Often mistaken for an aurora, airglow – greenish waves covering the sky and sometimes seen in the Highlands – is created in the upper atmosphere after ultraviolet radiation generated during daylight hours excites and fractures oxygen molecules. As the atoms recombine they emit energy as an amazing green glow.

blue and pink from nitrogen. Rare scarlet arises from oxygen high in the atmosphere reacting with the solar particles.

Aurora borealis

Dark, clear sky is essential for seeing auroras. Check for activity and locations on websites such as Aurora Watch UK. For best viewing choose a low horizon towards the north.

EXTRAORDINARY FACT

A GLOW NAMED STEVE

Steve, a rare thin purple ribbon light display, lasting about 20 minutes during an aurora returned spectacularly to Argyll in November 2023 and to the Highlands in October 2024. A fast-moving stream of extremely hot particles, scientists call it Strong Thermal Emission Velocity Enhancement. Its name Steve was inspired by the squirrel in the 2006 movie *Over the Hedge*.

BELOW ZERO
The shapes and sounds of snow and ice

For snow lovers in the Cairngorms most cherished are 'blue powder' days, when the sun is shining, the wind light and the snow 'virgin'. Wind-sculpted snow drifts, like iridescent coral reefs are also a delight. At the Cairngorm Mountain Railway station, 663 m (2,175 ft) above sea level, it snows on average for 76.2 days a year, with a depth of up to 3.2 m (10 ft); for the entire country it is 36 days. The Cairngorms are home to 'The Sphinx', a patch of snow first noted by mountaineers in the 1840s on Braeriach, the country's third highest mountain. It has melted only 10

According to folk legend a fairy man would ride sitting backwards on a deer to warn Highlanders of approaching snow.

times since the 1970s but has disappeared in eight summers since 2000. Visited in 1801 by Sarah Murray, the 'snow house' at Ciste Mhearad also persists late into the year. Ice is an everyday winter phenomenon, but most extraordinary when, as spindrift, it hisses as it dances on lofty thermals.

EXTRAORDINARY FACT

Like huge dinner plates up to 3 m (10 ft) across and 10 cm (4 in) thick, ice pancakes – circular blocks of ice – that can spin as they bump together are rare wonders seen in January 2024 at Brora in Sutherland and on a reservoir near Loch Lomond. As the water starts to freeze waves or currents make loose ice crystals stick together, forming 'frazil' a slushy ice. In the mountains, ice ridges like huge, blazing white feathers form when supercooled water droplets are blown onto an already freezing surface. With each successive blast more ice forms. In the mountains, wind compacts snow into 'wind slabs' which can be suddenly released as avalanches. Between 100 and 350 significant avalanches are reported in Scotland each year. Observing rime ice, formed by the rapid freezing of supercooled water and its behaviour is essential to avalanche prediction. Hair ice, masses of very thin strands of ice like fleeting, frozen candyfloss on rotting wood and visible at night and the early morning, is a rare and beautiful sight. It forms on water seeping out of the wood but only in the presence of a fungus named *Exidiopis effusa*, thought to produce a chemical that can stabilize the ice for several hours.

> **QUICK FACTS**
> **SOME SNOWY WORDS**
>
> • It is said that the Scots have more than 400 words for snow and how it behaves including:
>
> • *Spitters*: Small flakes of wind-driven snow (or rain).
>
> • *Bleffert*: A sudden, violent snowfall.
>
> • *Skelf*: A large snowflake.
>
> • *Flindrikin*: A small snow shower.
>
> • *Ewden-drift*: Snow drifted by the wind.
>
> • *Goor*: Broken ice and half-melted snow.

THE BITING CLOUDS
The scourge of the midge

'The midge is as big as a mountain' and 'there's little between a cow and a midge' run two old Scottish sayings. From May to September in the Highlands, and especially on peat moors, midges amass in millions like grey clouds, the females biting deer and cattle as well as humans. Traps set in August can accumulate a million midges in a single night; by one estimate Scotland

AMAZING FACT

THE MIGHTY MIDGE
According to legend midges drove away the Norwegian giant Thrim when he attempted to invade Scotland. Bonnie Prince Charlie is said to have been tormented by midges in his flight to Skye following defeat at Culloden in 1746.

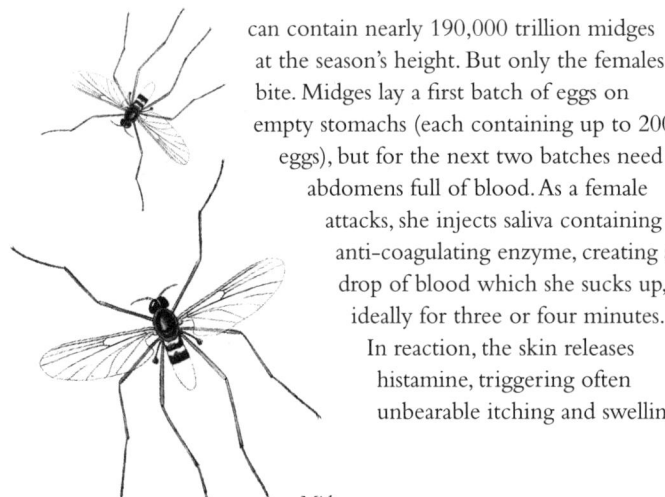

can contain nearly 190,000 trillion midges at the season's height. But only the females bite. Midges lay a first batch of eggs on empty stomachs (each containing up to 200 eggs), but for the next two batches need abdomens full of blood. As a female attacks, she injects saliva containing an anti-coagulating enzyme, creating a drop of blood which she sucks up, ideally for three or four minutes. In reaction, the skin releases histamine, triggering often unbearable itching and swelling.

Midges

EXTRAORDINARY FACT

In 1952 the University of Edinburgh set up a Midge Control Unit which now publishes daily midge forecasts using data from traps combined with detailed weather predictions. The forecast map is marked with circles numbered from 1 to 5; 1 and 2 mean mostly midge free but even level 3 can demand serious precautions. When considering a campsite, or a property for sale or rent, always check its position relative to the 'midge line'. Many holiday sites now have midge traps that mimic the reactions of human skin.

DID YOU KNOW?

Some people are lucky enough to have genes enabling them to produce large amounts of a natural midge repellent (a type of ketone). Favoured skin applied deterrents range from Marmite to eucalyptus oil, and current research is concentrated on the bog myrtle, but many swear by repellents containing picaridin which works by blocking the midge's antennae, or DEET. Avon's Skin So Soft Dry Oil Body Spray (not sold as a deterrent) is also popular.

Bog myrtle

QUICK FACTS

- The midge belongs to the insect order Diptera (two winged flies). The species most responsible for biting is *Culicoides impunctatus*.

- Midge larvae hatch within 24 hours, then burrow like earthworms, aerating the soil and assisting organic decomposition.

- Midges don't carry human pathogens but may transmit the blue tongue virus fatal to sheep.

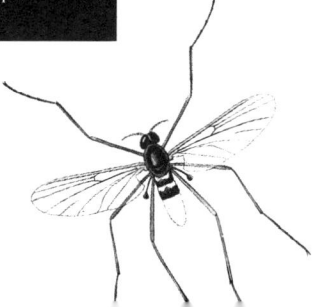

AS WHITE AS SNOW
Keeping safe – and fed – in winter

When snow falls on the mountains, three exceptional creatures may be detectable only by their footprints. The mountain hare (*Lepus timidus*), the rock ptarmigan (*Lagopus muta*) and the stoat (*Mustela erminea*) are all adapted to turn white in winter, but for different reasons. For hares and ptarmigans, camouflage from predators, notably raptors, is a necessity, but stoats, which catch and kill the hares, need to hide from their prey. But whiteness is never total. The hare's ears remain tipped with distinguishing

QUICK FACTS

- Ptarmigan are named from the Gaelic *tarmachan* for 'croaker' from their rattling calls, also likened to loudly ticking clocks. *Lagopus* means 'hare foot'.

- The 'p' in ptarmigan was added by the 17th century Scottish ornithologist Sir Robert Sibbald (1641-1722) thinking mistakenly that the word had Greek origins.

- Unlike stoats, mountain hares and ptarmigan are confined to Scotland. Like brown hares, mountain species are feared as shape shifters and witches in disguise.

EXTRAORDINARY FACT

Ptarmigan are grouse family members whose males have four different plumages through the year, females only three. In summer the bodies of both turn a dappled greyish green, disguising them as lichen covered stones; the wing feathers remain white. If disturbed, they will run with a rolling gait but can suddenly take off, rising high. In harsh weather they roost in rocky holes away from the prevailing wind. Ptarmigan feet are traditionally made into kilt pins conferring good luck.

black, and the ptarmigan's black beak and eyes stand out. The sinuous stoat, whose winter coat is named ermine, a fur used to adorn and insulate the robes of royalty and aristocracy since the 12th century, is visible only from its black nose, eye sockets and bushy tail tip. While stoats and hares are active by night, ptarmigan feed by day, their feathered feet acting like snowshoes as they probe for lichens, heather and moss. Similarly, mountain hares have large, splayed toes, helping them to run across snowy ground. Their leverets, often born in March when the weather is still harsh, are unusually protected with fur, but only around 20 per cent survive to adulthood.

Ptarmigan

THE SNOW BUNTING

Not pure white, despite its alternative names of snowflake, snow fowl and snow fleck, the tiny snow bunting (*Plectrophenax nivalis*) is one of nature's great survivors having even been seen at the North Pole and recorded as earth's most northerly breeding bird. As these winter visitors from the north take off in large flocks they create dramatic 'blizzards' of white wings and tail markings, although their plumage is more buff coloured in winter's depths. When, rarely, they breed in Scotland, nests in rock crevices are insulated with everything from mountain hares' fur to sheep's wool and even eagle feathers.

LAPLAND COMES TO THE CAIRNGORMS
Scotland's reindeer herd

In April 1952, two reindeer bulls and five cows disembarked in Scotland from a Swedish ship, the *SS Sarek*. Following quarantine they were released onto the Cairngorm plateau to graze over its sub-arctic terrain. Their arrival was the brainchild of reindeer herder Mikel Utsi and his wife, the Swedish-US anthropologist Dr Ethel Lindgren who had visited Scotland on their honeymoon in 1947 and been reminded of Lapland's reindeer pastures. Today the herd of around 150, split between the Cairngorms and the Cromdale hills near Glenlivet, survives for much of the year on a meagre diet of lichens, chiefly reindeer moss (a blueish green lichen branched like reindeer antlers) plus food supplements. In spring and summer willow, birch, grasses and birds' eggs top up their diet.

> **AMAZING FACT**
>
> **ALL AGLOW**
> To keep their nasal cavities warm, and to help them detect reindeer moss and other food, reindeer are endowed with extra blood vessels. This does make them glow a little, though almost certainly not as brightly as Rudolph.

Of all female deer, only reindeer sport antlers, but the growth pattern in males and females differs. While males shed their antlers in November and December, immediately after the rutting season, the females keep theirs until the spring, after their calves are born. So it is fair to conclude that Santa's reindeer are in fact females!

EXTRAORDINARY FACT

Reindeer (*Rangifer tarandus*) are extraordinarily adapted to cold and snow. Each hair of their fur is hollow, adding to its insulation, and further enhanced by the layering of long, dense hairs over a thick woolly undercoat. To help retain heat reindeer nostrils have a large surface area for warming air while their hooves, spongy in summer for walking on boggy ground, shrink and harden in autumn for gripping snow and ice. As reindeer walk their legs make clicking sounds produced by the action of tendon on bone and thought to help members of the herd stay close when poor weather reduces visibility.

QUICK FACTS

• Calves born each year are named according to specific themes including ice cream – hence Gelato, Magnum and Scoop.

• A fully grown male can weigh 150 kg and bear 1 m (3 ft) antlers.

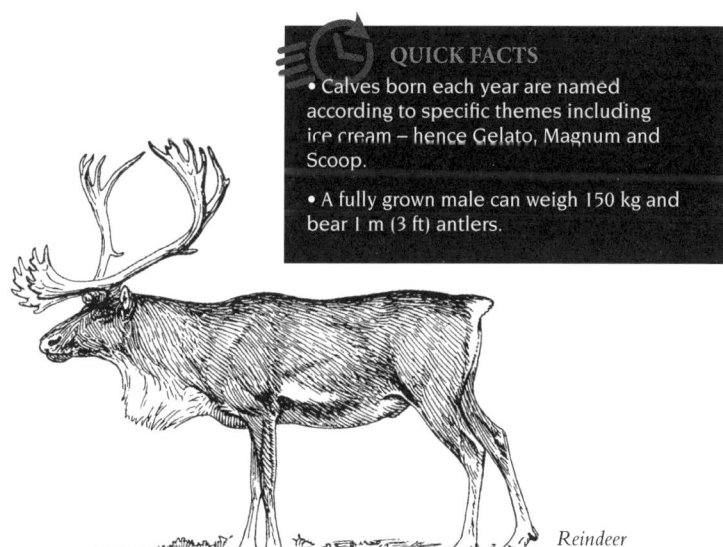

Reindeer

HISTORY IN THE ROCKS
Finding fossil treasures

The Isle of Skye is a fossil hunter's 'paradise', most famous for the Storr Lochs Monster, an almost perfect skeleton of an ichthyosaur 4 m (13 ft) long and 170 million years old. Discovered in 1966 as strings of fossilized vertebrae jutting from rock it remained entombed until 2015 when work began on its release. Acclaimed a new species, the pterosaur *Ceoptera evansae* was discovered on Skye in 2006. Many ammonites and belemnites that lived in shallow Jurassic seas, plus later remains of fish, lizards, turtles, crocodiles and early mammals are among its other treasures. Skye is also famous for its trilobites, the fossilized external skeletons of arthropods dating to the Cambrian 541 to 485 million years ago.

AMAZING FACT

THE OLDEST
About a billion years old, and looking like a small blob, the world's oldest fossil, a single-celled marine organism named *Bicellum brasieri*, was found in 2021 at Loch Torridon in the northwest Highlands. The Inner Hebridean Island Kerrera is home to the oldest millipede yet found, dating back 425 million years.

DID YOU KNOW?

From the southern uplands emerge graptolites, feathery remains of colonial sea creatures dating to the Ordovician (485 to 443 million years ago). Dura Den in Fife is a prime site for early fish from the Devonian (419-359 Ma). Footprints on the isle of Arran have been traced to *Chirotherium*, a dinosaur precursor from the Triassic (252-201 Ma).

QUICK FACTS

The south of Scotland has some excellent fossil hunting sites, but always check for access and permission. They include:

• Pentland Hills: Trilobites, corals, cephalopods and shellfish.

• Lady Burn, South Ayrshire: Renowned for starfish but also trilobites and varied Ordovician fossils.

• Glenmard Wood, South Ayrshire: Brachiopods and bivalves.

• Dobbs Linn, Dumfries and Galloway: Famous for its graptolites.

• Dalmellington Tip, East Ayrshire: Fish teeth and scales, coprolites (fossilized faeces), shells and plant remains in shale.

• Aldons Quarry: Trilobites, brachiopods and many other Ordovician fossils.

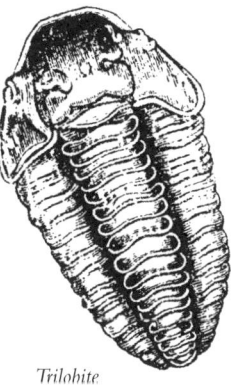

Trilobite

EXTRAORDINARY FACT

Now a Dumbarton village, 300 million years ago Bearsden was once a brackish lagoon where the famous 1 m (3 ft) Bearsden Shark thrived. Its carcass was quickly buried in thick mud but even as land masses moved and changed was never exposed to decaying air. When discovered in 1981 it was the best-preserved shark skeleton known. Now on display at the Hunterian Museum, Glasgow, part of its final meal is still in the stomach, plus blood vessel and muscle remnants.

ON TOP OF THE WORLD
Mighty mountains

It was an enormous crunch. Around 430 million years ago two ancient continents collided, creating Scotland's magnificent mountains. Originally layers of sea floor sediment, Moine rocks formed about 1,000 million years ago were heated and compressed forming a zone 200 km (124 miles) long from Sutherland to the Isle of Skye. Since then, volcanoes, glaciers and changing climates have continued to shape the landscape. Highest are the Cairngorms, Britain's largest granite mass, home to extraordinary wildlife ranging from imported reindeer to the rare Scottish crossbill (*Loxia scotica*), the UK's only endemic bird. Traces of past life come from caves such as the magical Bone Caves of Inchnadamph in Sutherland where geologists have found remains of creatures that once roamed the mountains including lynx, polar bears and arctic foxes.

AMAZING FACT

OF GREAT AGE
Some of the world's oldest rocks, the Lewisian Gneiss formed over 2 billion years ago are key components the Torridon Hills in the Northwest Highlands. Atop these is a massive layer made mostly of red sandstone 7,000 million years old, topped with shining white quartzite. Along the sides of three distinct mountain ranges, Beinn Alligin, Liathach and Beinn Eighe, the layers of rock make spectacular viewing.

Scottish crossbill

EXTRAORDINARY FACT

The most spectacular mountains of very many include:

• The Three Sisters: The peaks of Glencoe, Beinn Fhada, Gearr Aonach and Aonach Dub, are the names of three Campbell sisters who fell in love with rival MacDonalds but failed to survive, instead being turned to rock.

• Ben Lomond: A small Munro at 973 m (3,192 ft); a fabulous views of the loch below.

• Ben Macdui: Britain's second highest at 1,309 m (4,295 ft) and the Cairngorms highest set in a wild, challenging plateau. Snow may persist all year.

• The Five Sisters of Kintail: Peaks above Glen Sheil in the Western Highlands named from the legend of five sisters abandoned to spinsterhood, unlike their two married siblings. Deeply disappointed they asked a local wizard to transform them into mountains to preserve their beauty while they waited for husbands.

• Suilven, Sutherland: Only 731 m (92,398 ft); its Gaelic name means 'pillar mountain', but it is nicknamed the 'sugar loaf'. Part of a ridge formed of red sandstone.

• The Black Cuillin, Skye: Formed 60 million years ago from a collapsed volcano, now weathered to a dramatic jagged ridge.

Scotland's peaks are categorized by height:
- Munros: Named for Sir Hugh Munro (1856-1919) who in 1891 compiled a list of 282 peaks over 914.5 m (3,000 ft), 12 of them on Skye.
- Corbetts: 222 peaks between 762 m (2,500) and (914.5 m (3,000 ft) named for John Rooke Corbett (1876-1949) who first listed them in the 1920s. He was the fourth climber to complete the Munros.
- Donalds: Hills in the Lowlands over 762 m (2,500 ft); numbering 89 they were listed in 1935 by climber Percy Donald.
- Marilyns: 'Easy' Munros comprising any hill over 152 m (499 ft) with a drop of 150 m (492 ft) on all sides.

Sir Hugh Munro

THE HIGHEST PEAK

A giant volcano that collapsed inwards millions of years ago, at 1,345 m (4,413 ft) Ben Nevis in the Grampians is Britain's highest mountain. Its Gaelic name is **Beinn Nibheis**, *meaning 'the mountain with its head in the clouds' or 'venomous'. According to legend a resident giant once threw boulders from the summit at anyone who dared to climb it. Sitting atop the mountain on her throne is the giant Cailleach, goddess of winter, a fearsome one-eyed hag with white hair, blue skin and rust-red teeth, who shaped mountain ranges with her magic hammer. In winter she dusts the peaks with snow and frost but protects deer and other animals.*

QUICK FACTS

• Queen Victoria hiked to the summit of Ben Macdui in 1859, aged 40. She declared it '... had a sublime and solemn effect, so wild, so solitary – no one but ourselves and our little party there ... I had a little whisky and water, as the people declared pure water would be too chilling.'

• According to myth the Cuillin ranges were formed when the sun flung her spear into the ground, creating a huge, expanding blister that eventually burst.

Ben Nevis

WHERE EAGLES DARE
Magnificent raptors

Today you are more likely to thrill to eagles circling on the air currents of Scotland's skies than at any time in the last three centuries. And this is true for both the golden eagle (*Aquila chrysaetos*) and the white-tailed or sea eagle (*Haliaeetus albicilla*) now increasingly seen inland. Almost as soon as Hogmanay is past golden eagles will begin checking out their eyries – usually on cliff ledges but sometimes atop tall trees – to make sure that their old nests are fit for the new breeding year and adding sticks that can extend a nest

★ AMAZING FACT ★

POTENT SYMBOLS
White-tailed eagle remains found in Orkney tombs lend them religious significance. The Gaelic name *iolaire suile na grein* means 'the eagle with the sunlit eye'. Golden eagles, said to be able to look at the sun without going blind, have a long history as symbols of power and clan chiefs still decorate their bonnets with three eagle feathers. In old age, it is said, a golden eagle will fly so close to the sun that its feathers catch fire and will then dive into the sea, restoring its youth as if by magic.

Golden eagle

to make it a metre (3 ft) wide and 80 cm (2½ ft) deep. Once fully grown fledgelings join their parents swooping for mammals such as rabbits, hares, foxes and a variety of birds, including grouse. While golden eagles favour the mountains their white-tailed cousins, while also reusing old nesting sites, favour sheltered sea and inland lochs and habitually nest in trees. Ahead of mating pairs grapple in mid air and plummet cartwheeling towards the ground. Fish are key foods, but they also take rabbits and hares and will even steal food from otters.

QUICK FACTS

• Eagles are most visible on sunny days. Watch out for ravens mobbing them if there is a carcass nearby.

• Findhorn Valley in the Highlands is one of the best places to see golden eagles and a variety of other raptors.

• Islands such as Harris, Mull, Rum and Skye are ideal for viewing both golden and white-tailed eagles.

• White-tailed eagles have been recorded at Loch Lomond and Loch Ness.

SPOT THE DIFFERENCE

For the birdwatcher the 'jizz' is key to distinguishing golden from white-tailed eagles. In flight, golden eagles are more like buzzards, their wings held in a characteristic V shape, while white-tailed eagles have a more flapping flight, usually lower in the sky. Tails of white-tailed eagles are shorter, their wings broader and with a wider span; their beaks are also heavier.

White-tailed eagle

> **EXTRAORDINARY FACT**
>
> Golden eagles were once persecuted for their reputation for killing lambs, a practice now outlawed, although birds will certainly take the carrion of dead sheep and deer and stillborn lambs. The rise in golden eagle populations has been hugely helped by the reduction in use of pesticides, but has also been favoured by the South of Scotland Eagle Project which has transported chicks south from the north and the islands to a secret location near to where breeding appears to have been successful. White-tailed eagles remain lamb takers but Maremmas, an ancient breed of sturdy thick-coated sheepdogs used since Roman times to scare off wolves and bears, are now being trained to scare off the birds.

TIMBER!
The world of pines

The Roman naturalist Pliny the Elder called it 'the Wood of Caledon', today it is the Caledonian Forest, which reached its peak about 7,000 years ago. As the climate warmed and vast blanket bogs formed, the forest that once covered over 15,000 sq m (60,000 sq miles) began to retreat, both naturally and from human activity including burning and grazing. Today it covers a mere 1.80 sq km (70 sq miles) mainly in the central and northeastern Grampians and in the northern and western Highlands. Yet this is still a perfect place to appreciate the soaring grandeur of the Scots pine (*Pinus sylvestris*), Scotland's national tree since 2014 and its only native timber producer, able to thrive in poor, acid soils. As habitations became established, its immensely strong timber, known as 'red deal' became invaluable. In time its trunks were made into ships' masts, water pipes, railway sleepers, telegraph poles, and were sources of charcoal and paper, of tar and turpentine. Its high resin content makes the wood extremely slow to decay, and dry, resin-rich fir cones could easily kindle a fire. But pines were never felled when the moon was waning as this was thought to drain resin away. Heavy rain can interact with the sap in pine tree bark, creating a soapy foam that drips down the trunk, collecting near tree bases.

★ AMAZING FACT ★

ANCIENT AND MYSTERIOUS

Scotland's most ancient pine, estimated to be over 565 years old, has been saved at Glen Loyne in the northwest Highlands. Alongside such relics, vibrant seedlings are protected with fencing to keep voracious deer away. Single pines were used to mark the burial places of warriors, heroes and chieftains and at Doon Hill, Aberfoyle, the ghost of Revd Robert Kirk, allegedly abducted by fairies in 1692, is said to wander near the Fairy Tree pine in which his spirit rests.

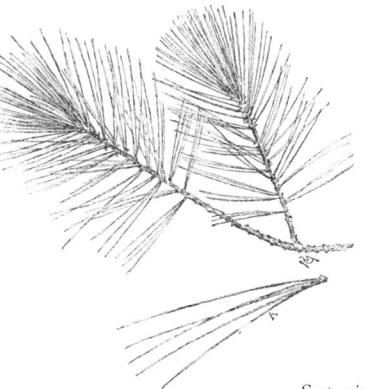

Scots pine

EXTRAORDINARY FACT

Although less diverse than other woodlands, the Caledonian Forest is home to Scottish crossbills (*Loxia curvirostra*), with sweet, trilling voices, brilliantly adept at teasing seeds from pinecones with their pincerlike beaks. Capercaillie and black grouse are at home here, along with red squirrels and occasional wildcats, but most successful are the 172 insect species that thrive among the trees, including longhorn beetles, and pine weevil larvae that burrow into the wood. Pine beauty moths are among the insects whose caterpillars feed on pine needles; these become, in turn, food for wood ants – supplementing the nectar they obtain from abundant aphids – so helping to protect trees from defoliation. On the forest floor are mats of the rare, protected twinflower (*Linnea borealis*), named from the two flowers that bloom on slender Y-shaped stems. On summer nights it emits a wonderful lilac-like scent.

QUICK FACTS

- A Scots pine at Muirward Wood, Perthshire has the largest trunk. Measuring 6 m (19½ ft) across, it is split into three.

- Norway spruce wood, tough and elastic, is known as 'white deal' or 'violin wood' from its colour and sound transmitting quality.

- Scots pine roots were traditionally used to make baskets, ropes and even candles that were deemed lucky when lit.

- Derivations of *giuthas*, the Gaelic word for pine, can be found in place names such as Dalguise and Kingussie.

- When wearing tartan was outlawed following the Jacobite Rebellion of 1745 the Clan MacGregor began wearing Scots pine in defiance.

Non-native pine trees with massive presence include:
- The Sitka spruce (*Picea sitchensis*), comprising around 58 per cent of Scotland's forests and named for an Alaskan city, was first grown from seed brought to Europe in 1831 by the Scots plant hunter David Douglas (1799-1834). They are additionally rain and salt tolerant, disease resistant and able to grow up to 1.5 m (5 ft) a year its white wood proved ideal for everything from paper making to boat building and musical instruments. Tree creepers, siskins and coal tits nest in its dense foliage but sitka woodlands discourage biodiversity.
- David Douglas also brought the noble fir (A*bies procera*) from Washington and Oregon, with striking blueish grey needles, and the eponymous Douglas fir (*Pesudotsuga menziesii*). Scotland's tallest Douglas firs stand at Reelig Glen near Inverness including Dughall Mor, the 'big dark stranger'.
- The lodgepole pine (*Pinus contorta* var. *latifolia*) was used by First Nation Americans to support wigwams. From 1855 its tolerance of poor soils quickly made it a favourite.
- Nordmann firs (A*bies nordmanniana*) from the Caucasus and aromatic Fraser firs (A. *fraseri*) originally from the Appalachians, both prized for their 'no drop' needles, are grown extensively as Christmas trees. The Norway spruce (*Picea abies*) is a traditional choice.
- The deciduous (*Larix decidua*) arrived from central Europe 400 years ago. Black grouse feed on its buds and immature cones; cone scales are key food for larch tortrix moth caterpillars. From 2010 millions have been felled in southern Scotland to help eliminate the deadly fungal disease *Phytophthora ramorum*.

A FOREST REFUGE
Home for the elusive red squirrel

Red squirrel

A flash of fiery red among the conifers, whether in Galloway, Argyll or the Caledonian forests never fails to excite. A dainty red squirrel (*Sciurus vulgaris*), may even pause and look down with beady black eyes as it searches acrobatically for food, using its bushy tail for balance. Unlike many mammals, red squirrels can only store a little body fat, so must search actively all day for the pinecones, and seeds comprising their diet, supplemented by bark and berries. In

EXTRAORDINARY FACT

During the Highland Clearances red squirrels virtually disappeared from Scotland but introductions were made from the 1770s, and by 1900 were even given vermin status and regularly stoned or shot. Since the grey squirrel's arrival in England from America in 1876, which competed aggressively for food and nesting sites, reds have gradually been pushed farther north. Today, around 75 per cent of Britain's 160,000 reds are in Scotland but even here remain threatened by greys, which transport the squirrelpox virus.

autumn they bury pine cones in shallow stores as winter larders. Red squirrels reside and raise their young (kits) in dreys, untidy spheres of twigs lined with moss, grasses, leaves and fur set into branch forks. Individuals may even have several dreys, mothers moving kits between them.

QUICK FACTS
- Red squirrels hive double jointed ankles, enhancing their agility.
- An adult weighs only around 250 g (9 oz) but can jump 2 m (6 ft).
- Reds are Britain's only native squirrels.
- The red squirrel features on the 2024 King Charles III two pence coin.

- Red squirrels receive some protection from competition from grey squirrels by the highland boundary fault running from Arran to Helensburgh whose gorges and waterfalls they find difficult to cross.
- They are additionally safeguarded by the vigilance of dedicated naturalists.
- A pinecone nibbled by a red squirrel looks like an apple core. To eat hazelnuts they crack the shells in half.
- Red squirrels do not hibernate but store large supplies of nuts. They have an exceptional sense of smell and can not only find food buried in deep snow but detect a rotten nut without having to waste energy opening it.

THE GREAT ACROBATS
Agile pine martens

They emerge at dusk, leaping from branch to branch, covering horizontal distances of up to 4 m (13 ft), or dropping dramatically 20m (65 ft) from tree to ground in search of small mammals such as mice and voles, birds' eggs or nutritious berries. But handsome, intelligent pine martens (*Martes martes*), relatives of stoats and weasels with lustrous brown faces and creamy fur bibs stretching from throat to chest, have mixed reputations. As protected species they

DID YOU KNOW?

The creamy bib of every pine marten is unique in shape and size, making it possible to identify and study individual animals.

EXTRAORDINARY FACT

In summer and early autumn, pine martens devour bilberries, blackberries and rowan berries, turning their droppings (scats) a definitive blue or red. The scats are deposited on rocks or prominent logs, marking out their large territories, which for each individual extend between 86 and 166 hectares (212 and 410 acres). Fresh scats are slimy, being bound together with mucus, and can contain fur, bones and feathers.

are omnivores notorious for devouring the eggs of rare birds such as capercaillie, small birds and even red squirrels and their kits. Increasingly bold, even near habitations, they make dens in rooves, indulge in killing sprees in chicken coops and rob garden bird feeders. However, they are also partial to grey squirrels. In the 19th century, when considered vermin, their pelts were used to line magistrates' robes.

QUICK FACTS

- Pine martens are similar in size to small domestic cats. Males are roughly a third bigger than females.

- Individuals of both sexes are solitary. Cat-like yowls, heard in summer, mark the mating season. Litters of up to five cubs are born in spring.

- Pine martens are the only mustelids with semi-retractable claws, making them able to climb trees.

- The estimated Scottish population is around 3,700 adults.

Pine marten

ALL FOR SHOW
Mating rituals of the capercaillie and black grouse

Click, click, pop, pop, whistle, grunt – at dawn in March and April, in the depths of the Caledonian pine forest these are the rare, unmistakable sounds of two male capercaillie or 'great grouse' (*Tetrao urogallus*) in action which can be heard as far as 300 m (1,000 ft) away. With their scarlet eyebrows, and plumage iridescent in black, brown and purple, they approach each other with feathers and tails fanned out and necks outstretched as they face off, observed by a bevvy of females perched in the trees around this arena known as the lek. After a few hours, once a winner is obvious, the females will descend to mate with him.

Black grouse (*Tetrao tetrix*) also perform spectacular leks in open areas close to forests. Usually 6 to 10 but sometimes up to 30 males perform, each with a raised lyre-shaped white tail and a pair of startling red 'eyebrows' contrasting with their black feathers. As they peck and kick each other, neck feathers raised, they make cooing sounds called 'rookooking' which can carry for over 400 m (¼ mile). Each male has its own territory; the higher his status the nearer he is to the centre. The watching females or 'grey hens' are small and insignificantly mottled in brown with black bars.

QUICK FACTS

• Only well fed males have the energy for lekking. Both capercaillie and black grouse feed on pine needles, heather and berries. Capercaillie also eat small pine cones.

• Following successful breeding a female black grouse will stay faithful to her mate.

• Capercaillie rarely live beyond 3½ years.

• Lekking birds are increasingly threatened by thoughtless tourists, some even taking selfies.

Capercaillie

EXTRAORDINARY FACT

Capercaillie, the world's largest grouse, were abundant in Scotland 150,000 years ago but numbers reduced in the Middle Ages and by 1785 they were extinct. New populations were brought from Scandinavia in the 1830s but the 20,000 individuals of the 1970s are now reduced to around 550. Among the threats to their survival are the removal of woodland habitats and, within them, the destruction of understorey shelters by deer. Birds are also killed by colliding with fences erected within woods to control deer movement. Predation by pine martens (a protected species) and wetter springs can both be fatal to chicks.

MORE THAN JUST MUSHROOMS
Into the world of fungi

In their many shapes and forms – and hidden below ground – fungi are vital to the ecosystem, exchanging vital nutrients with plants, decomposing and recycling dead vegetation and providing food and shelter for animals of all sizes, especially in woodlands. Scotland is home to more than 12,000 fungal species but is internationally renowned for its waxcaps, named for their shiny tops. Popping up in grassland in summer and autumn they have an array of descriptive names including scarlet; crimson; pink; golden; blackening; glutinous; oily; honey; date-coloured; green parrot; and simply splendid. Critical for waxcaps (many but not all in the genus *Hygrocybe*) is soil that is nutrient poor. The chief threats to their survival are disruption of the soil and fertilizer of any kind.

AMAZING FACT

WHO EATS WHO?
In ancient hazel woodland, but only in the cleanest air, the orange hazel gloves fungus *(Hypocreopsis rhododendri)* wraps itself with finger-like projections around branches. Beneath it is the pitch-black glue crust fungus *(Hymenochaete corrugate)* on which it feeds. Meanwhile the gummy glue crust is decaying and absorbing food from branches, which it catches in its tarry grasp as they fall, holding them bizarrely horizontal.

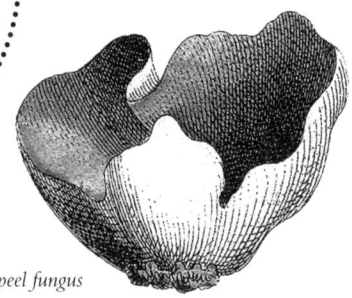

Orange peel fungus

EXTRAORDINARY FACT

WHAT'S IN A NAME?

From a cast of thousands, some amazingly named and extraordinary fungi include:

• Dead man's fingers (*Xylaria polymorpha*): Like swollen blackened fingers protruding from the ground. Usually beneath beech.

• Amethyst deceiver (*Laccaria amethystina*): Named from its wide variety of shapes and sizes and deep purple colour. Long stemmed and edible.

• Orange peel fungus (*Aleuria aurantia*): Stemless, curled bright caps whose shape is true to their name. Found near woodland paths; edible.

• Green elf cup or blue stain fungus (*Chlorociboria aeruginascens*): Unmistakable disks of bright turquoise on decaying deciduous wood. Highly poisonous.

• Devil's tooth or bleeding tooth fungus (*Hydnellum peckii*): A white cap dotted with droplets of bright red liquid which may also appear on the underside. Rare; confined to the Caledonian forest. Edible, tastes hot like chilli.

• Hen of the woods or dancing mushroom (*Grifola frondosa*): A large mass of interlocking flat lobed grey fronds in different shades. Usually found at the base of oaks. According to a Japanese legend, Buddhist nuns and woodcutters once met on a mountain trail, where they discovered it and were so thrilled that they danced to celebrate. Edible.

• Chicken of the woods (*Laetiporus sulphureus*): Bright yellow multi-bracketed fungus. Avoid eating; always poisonous when growing on yew.

GOOD TO EAT

Many fungi are desirably edible, but always double check identities and forage conservatively. Prime harvest is the rich, nutty cep (*Boletus edulis*) or penny bun, named for its bread like brown cap that favours pine forests. Woodlands also yield apricot scented chanterelles (*Cantharellus cibarius*) and similar tasting hedgehog mushrooms (*Hydnum repandum*), named for the distinctive spines clustered beneath their pale brown leathery caps. The bark-growing beefsteak fungus (*Fistulina hepatica*) tasting more like liver than steak, is edible but highly acidic and when cut oozes a blood like liquid. At pine tree bases prized cauliflower fungi (*Sparassis crispa*) can appear yearly, their twisted branching lobes a creamy yellow.

Beefsteak fungus

QUICK FACTS

- Ancient oaks are home to the rare, oak polypore (*Buglossoporus quercinus*), an orangey multilayered bracket fungus. Removing any part of it is illegal.

- Oyster mushrooms (*Pleurotus ostreatus*) are edible but often stuffed full of maggots.

- 'Green oak', wood infected by green elf fungus, was prized by woodworkers in the 18th and 19th centuries who used it for inlays in decorative boxes.

Walk in woodlands at night and you may see bioluminescent or foxfire fungi glowing blueish green. They include the bitter oysterling (*Panellus stipticus*) and the rare jack o'lantern (*Omphalotus olearius*).

ON THE WING
Bats and butterflies, dragon and damselflies

After a great decline in numbers during the 20th century, due largely to the destruction of vast areas of woodland, bats now have protected status in Scotland. All are nighttime hunters, using echolocation to detect their insect prey, but most of the country's ten species live in the lowlands, with numbers declining northward and westward. Among the rarest is the tiny whiskered bat (*Myotis mystacinus*) with long fur, weighing only around 5 g (less than ¼ oz) favouring clearings, hedges and streams rich in flies, although they will also take moths and winged beetles. Moths are also the preferred food of 'whispering' bats, the common brown long-eared species (*Plecotus auritus*) whose echolocation is virtually silent. As they hunt they move slowly, ears erect, eating small prey on the wing but taking larger items to tree perches, always feeding upside down. Unusually active in the early evening are handsome purple hairstreak butterflies (*Favonius quercus*), found patchily in the southwest and central countryside but rarely seen since they fly

Long-eared bat

near the tops of oak trees. Their dark wings are marked in pale purple. Flying by day are Scotland's many butterflies, not least the widespread Scotch argus (*Erebia epiphron*), most often seen in grasslands. Its dark, velvety upper sides open in the sun to reveal orange bands bearing distinctive dark spots, each with a central white dot.

> **AMAZING FACT**
>
> **SWIFT AND LOUD**
>
> The noctule (*Nyctalus noctula*) is Scotland's fastest, noisiest and largest bat. It can reach 48 km/h (30 mph) and its echolocation is audible to the human ear. Largest individuals can weigh 35 g (1¼ oz). Located in the south, they emerge before sunset and roost and hibernate in trees.

EXTRAORDINARY FACT

Among Scotland's rarest butterflies are some of the skippers, named for their rapid skittering flight as they move from flower to flower and sudden darts to intercept other insects, among them:

• Essex skipper (*Thymelicus lineola*): Found only near Lockerbie in Dumfries and Galloway. Has distinctive black undersides to its antennae. Named from its county of discovery in 1888.

• Dingy skipper (*Erynnis tages*): Not as dull as its name suggests, with prettily mottled wings. Found only in the northeast and southwest (including around Loch Ness). Caterpillars feed exclusively on bird's foot trefoil.

• Chequered skipper (*Carterocephalus palaemon*): Lives exclusively in Lochaber and north Argyll in damp grassy habitats at woodland edges. Wings are distinctively patterned in brown and with creamy orange blotches. Caterpillars are slow to develop.

ONLY IN SCOTLAND

*Always favouring watery locations, and emerging when days start to warm, are species of British dragon and damselflies found only in Scotland. Loch Garten is the best place to see the delicate northern damselfly (***Coenagrion hastulatum***), its abdomen marked in alternate sections of greenish blue and black, and the small white-faced darter (***Leucorrhinia dubi***), a dragonfly whose face is actually a cream colour. Glen Affric is favoured by those searching for the northern emerald (***Somatochlora arctica***) with an abdomen in dark, metallic green, which not only patrols the water surface but will fly high up into the trees to find insect food. Here too lives the azure hawker (***Aeshna caerulea***), its abdomen brightly spotted in turquoise blue. Often found on boggy moorlands it will also bask on rocks and trees. The only male dragonflies coloured black when mature – the black darters (***Sympetrum striolatum***) – also favour of boggy ground (young males and females are pale yellow with black stripes). Exclusive to Scotland are the Highland variants which are blackest of all.*

Damselfly

QUICK FACTS

• Both damsel and dragonflies have two wings, but dragonflies are larger and always hold their wings at right angles, not close to the body.

• Very few bats inhabit the islands.

• The chequered skipper became extinct in England in the 1970s but has now been reintroduced.

> Unlike other butterflies the large heath (*Coenonympha tullia*), found mostly in boggy areas at up to 610 m (2,000 ft), will perch on cotton grass and sedge, and take to the wing even in cloudy conditions as long as the temperature is 14°C (57°F). In windy weather they will stay very close to the ground. The caterpillars may take up to two years to develop. Of its three subspecies, the one found in Scotland lacks the distinctive eye spots on the grey and orange wings of the more southern types.

HIDDEN WOODLAND GEMS
The extraordinary temperate rainforest

Among nature's greatest marvels are Scotland's unique temperate Celtic rainforests, comprising oak, ash, birch, pine and hazel. This Atlantic woodland of Argyll and the west Highlands flourishes because the climate is hyper-oceanic, that is, extraordinarily wet and humid but mild. What makes these forests remarkable is not just the ancient trees, often weirdly contorted, but the epiphytic mosses, lichens and ferns growing on them – and on boulders of all shapes and sizes – shining in shades of green, blue and grey even in winter's depths. Come spring, flowers abound, with wild garlic, primroses, bluebells and dog violets creating swathes of colour. Increasingly rare migrant wood warblers and pied flycatchers nest here, and the

Pied flycatcher

spring air resounds with the calls of willow warblers and chiffchaffs. To date over 850 species of flying insects have been identified, among them the endangered chequered skipper butterfly and pearl bordered fritillary. Resident mammals include badgers, pine martens, red squirrels and wildcats. And of course there are midges.

Scotland's rainforest covers 2 per cent of its woodlands, a total of 30,000 hectares (74,000 acres), but only 20 per cent of the area with the climatic conditions in which it could thrive. Tree felling, and the introduction of non-native pines are constant threats, but forests are also in great danger from grazing deer and, despite their floral beauty, rampant and invasive rhododendrons, escapees from Victorian gardens that threaten to choke the forests. Because they absorb water direct from the air, mosses and other bryophytes, and lichens, are endangered by air pollution.

EXTRAORDINARY FACT

- The rainforest is a perfect habitat for mosses, liverworts and hornworts (bryophytes), our oldest land plants; a single stretch of woodland can contain hundreds of species. Mosses range from the large, grasslike greater fork moss (*Dicranum majus*) to the tiny humps of greater pincushion (*Ptychomitrium polyphyllum*) and rusty bow (*Dicranodontium subporodictyon*).

- Even more intruiging are the liverworts, small plants with flattened 'leaves' – flat stems covered with overlapping scales that can only survive when wet. Their name dates to Medieval times when, from their shape, they were boiled in wine and used to treat liver disorders. In the rainforest they range from the prickly featherwort (*Plagiochila spinulosa*), favouring damp ravines, to the bright green, moss like western featherwort (*P. heterophylla*), a rarity elsewhere in Europe.

- Many ferns festoon the forest floor but also grow from trees and rocks. Most minute are the filmy ferns. Just two species survive here, both identified by the 19th century botanist William Wilson (1799-1871), the rarer, fragile Tunbridge (*Hymenophyllum tunbrigense*) and the more common eponymous Wilson's filmy fern (*H. wilsonii*).

STARS OF THE FOREST

*More than 500 different lichens encrust trunks and branches in the woodland, each made of 'marriages' between fungi and, usually, algae. The aptly named tree lungwort (**Lobaria pulmonaria**), its scaly bright green lobes dotted with chestnut coloured, spore-baring discs, is a key indicator of an ancient forest. Its close relative, 'lob scrob' (**L. scrobiculata**) is a gunmetal blue. With white 'teeth' on their undersides dog lichens (**Peltigera canina**) were once sold as a cure for rabies. Much rarer and decidedly bizarre are the jelly lichens. Like the green* **Collema fasciculare** *they look as if they are covered in octopus suckers – in fact their fruiting bodies. Adding to the lichen rainbow is the blue jelly-skin lichen (**Leptogium cyanescens**). Large scallop-like forms, growing flat against branches typify the felt lichens such as* **Degelia plumbea**, *which can be any shade from grey to blueish black or brown. Very small overlapping scales typify the shingle lichens. The red-eyed shingle lichen (**Pannaria rubiginosa**) is grey-blue dotted with reddish brown fruiting bodies while the* **Sticta** *species smell like rotting fish when wet. Rarest of all is the smooth, thin white script lichen* **Graphis alboscripta**, *which has only ever been found on hazels in Scotland's rainforest.*

Tree lungwort

QUICK FACTS

- Lichens grey when dry can turn green once hydrated.
- Many lichens are aptly named, among them specklebelly, tailed-loop, green satin and dragon-skin.
- Hay-scented buckler ferns stay green all winter.
- Dyes for Harris tweed traditionally came from lichens.
- Tawny owls, siskins, woodpeckers and redwings are among other forest birds.
- Badgers make extensive setts in the forest.
- Acorns and hazelnuts are key food for jays and red squirrels.
- Over the centuries, the forests have been important sources of as timber and fuel; bark was used for tanning leather.
- Search Scotland's National Nature Reserves for the best sites to visit.

THE VALLEYS OF TIME
Glorious glens

Their mood can change almost instantly with the weather, and every glen – named from the Gaelic for 'steep-sided valley' – has its unique character. Most are long and many U-shaped, betraying their post glacial origins. Largest and most significant is the Great Glen, the 100 km (62 mile) fault line cutting the country in two between Fort William and Inverness, formed in a geological strike slip in which the rocks moved sideways. Also a magnet for geologists is Glen Tilt in Perthshire, where the river tumbles over rocks formed

QUICK FACTS

Scotland has more than 40 glens. These make exceptional visits:

• Glen Etive, Highland: Said to be the most scenic 19 km (12 miles) of countryside with mountains and moorlands, and clear, sparking lochs. The perfect pyramidal peak of Buachaille Etive Mor is among the most photographed mountains. Ian Fleming (1908-64), creator of James Bond, once owned a lodge here; with nearby Glen Coe it features in the movie *Skyfall*. The River Etive provides popular kayaking challenges.

• Glen Nevis, Highland: Home to Steall Falls, one of the three highest waterfalls in Scotland and access to Ben Nevis. Varied and accessible woodland trails rich in lichens; 75 species have been found here, 33 of them rare in the UK.

• Glen Derry, Highland: Set in heather moorland and pine forests. Haven for red squirrels. Great views, including Braemar, from Beinn Bhreac with its twin summits.

• Glen Lyon, Perth and Kinross: At 55 km (34 miles), Scotland's longest enclosed glen, celebrated by Sir Walter Scott (1771-1832). Long inhabited it was once the home of early Christian monks.

• Glen Affric, Highland: Ancient Caledonian pinewoods survive here, but also deciduous trees such as aspen, birch, willow and alder. Home to rare lichens and four species of wintergreen.

• Glen Cova: Dundee & Angus: Dramatic cliffs and waterfalls in a quiet glen whose surrounding hills and Munro contain many alpine flowers. Renowned as the territory of cattle thieves and whisky smugglers.

when molten lava forced its way into the side cracks in a fault then solidified to form granite. It was their discovery by the pioneer geologist James Hutton (1726-97) in 1785 that led to his then revolutionary theory of Plutonism – the idea that the geological time scale is incredibly long (contradicting that of Neptunism, claiming rocks precipitated out of water). And not all are remote. Glencorse in the Pentland Hills, vibrant in spring with yellow, butter-scented gorse is only minutes south of Edinburgh's city borders. Glens are ideal locations for nature lovers to spot red deer, mountain hares and wildcats, plus ptarmigans, eagles and ospreys. However much of the ancient woodlands that once covered the hillsides has now disappeared.

HAUNTING HISTORY, RARE BEAUTY
Deep and narrow, and enclosed by looming mountainous often swathed in cloud, Glen Coe the 'glen of weeping' never fails to inspire. Add to this the history of the 1692 massacre, when 38 MacDonalds were slain, and its location in films ranging from **Harry Potter** *to* **Braveheart** *and* **Skyfall**, *and this breathtaking landscape is an inevitable visitor magnet creating intense pressure on a precious natural environment. Around 420 million years ago a super volcano erupted forming a subsidence caldera in which a cauldron was formed by the sinking of the earth's crust. As this happened, magma was forced to the surface around its edges, as can still be seen in the layers of volcanic lava on Bidean nam Bian. Around the glen the peaks and plateaus are home to rare alpine flowers, notably the rare and protected drooping saxifrage (***Saxifraga cernua***).*

> Not all glens are on the mainland. Two spectacular island locations are:
> - Glen Sligachan, Skye: Divides the rugged Black and Red Cuillin mountains; filled with rushing burns and many small lochs. A great place to see both golden and sea eagles.
> - Glen Meavaig Outer Hebrides: Home of the North Harris Eagle Observatory, included in the Outer Hebrides Birds of Prey Trail. Undisturbed territory lacking predators such as foxes provides highly favourable breeding conditions for golden eagles. Boggy areas are rich in carnivorous sundews and butterworts.

Glen Coe

MONARCHS OF THE GLENS
Deer in their thousands

Summer is past. Now magnificent red deer stags (*Cervus elephus*) begin departing their all male groups and start herding harems of up to 20 females (hinds), all reaching their height of fertility. The hair around the stags' necks has grown into a thick mane and their massive bone antlers, measuring up to 1 metre (3 ft) across, are now fully formed. By mid October they are ready to defend their harem, roaring loudly to keep the hinds in check (some will be tempted to wander off and mate with younger males) before the rut in which competing, intruding stags will be fended off in violent

In the Highlands, red deer were dubbed 'fairy cattle' from the belief that fairies milked them at night. Because of their likeness to tree branches and their ability to regrow, stags' antlers are ancient symbols of fertility and rebirth. Lord of the Beasts, the Celtic horned god Cernunnos, was traditionally depicted with stags' horns.

QUICK FACTS

- The red deer, a true British native, is the largest deer species in the UK.

- A 'Royal' stag has 12 points to its antlers.

- Deer belong to no one while alive, but the right to take or kill them lies with the owner of the land where they are found.

- In Gaelic *bùiridh* (*BOOR-ee*) describes both the roaring, bellowing, wailing and growling of rutting.

- Some 110,000 wild deer are culled every year to control their numbers.

AMAZING FACT

APPETITE FOR ANTLERS

Red deer stags cast their antlers in March and April and begin growing new, usually larger ones, a process taking around 100 days. They will chew the old ones to boost the dietary calcium often sparse in Highland soils. Stags will rub off, and may even eat, the soft skin or velvet on the new growth in July when it dies naturally, helping to mature antlers for the rut. Cast antlers are free to collect and, from buttons to knife handles and works of art, have countless uses.

antler-to-antler ruts before the winner mates with all his hinds. During this time, which can literally be life or death, the stags barely eat and can lose up to 15 per cent of their body weight. Losers may even die from their injuries. The most fertile stags are upwards of eight years old; very few live to 30. The peak of calving is mid June, hinds rarely giving birth to twins. Although they can adapt to life on moors and hills, red deer prefer forests and woodlands where food is more plentiful.

'The Monarch of the Glen', created by English painter and Queen Victoria's favourite Sir Edwin Landseer (1802-73) in 1851 depicting a magnificent stag, was originally commissioned to hang in London's Palace of Westminster. Once completed, however, no money was forthcoming, and it was initially sold to a private collector. Subsequent transactions led to it trademarking such products as Pears Soap, Baxter's Royal Game Soup, Challenge Butter and Dewar's 'the Monarch' whisky. In 2017 it was finally bought by the National Galleries of Scotland.

EXTRAORDINARY FACT

Over a million deer live in Scotland (now being tracked and counted by drones), and are regarded with mixed emotions, as is the annual deer cull. Centuries ago, red deer were a vital source of food, clothing (from their hides) and tools, but as forests were cleared their numbers decreased. Today all deer are threats to Scotland's precious Celtic rainforest and moorland ecosystems, and are hosts to ticks, transmitters of Lyme disease.

As well as the reds three other species inhabit the land:

- Roe deer (*Capreolus capreolus*): Britain's most common deer, distinguished by pale, tailless rumps, browse freely on low growing plants, small shrubs and young trees. They roam everywhere but the Western and Northern Isles and are absent from Arran and Mull. Males (bucks) are usually solitary, guarding distinct territories, but may gather in small groups in winter.

- Fallow deer (*Dama dama*): Introduced by the Normans in the 11th century. They have spotted coats, black and white tails, and white rumps outlined in black. A fallow fawn was almost certainly the model for Bambi.

- Sika deer (*Cervus nippon*): Arrived from Asia as 'ornamentals' in the 1860s. Favouring coniferous forests they can do considerable damage and will hybridize with red deer, their close relations.

Sika deer

AUTUMN ABUNDANCE
Berries of many kinds

Some are tastier than others, but late summer and autumn bring an abundance of berries beside the common blackberry. On heaths, open woods and trails, wild raspberries (*Rubus idaeus*), with fruits smaller and sharper tasting than their cultivated relatives are common. Their scientific name means 'bramble of Mount Ida' from the Greek myth that Ida, the nurse of young Zeus wishing to calm his sorrows with a white fruit, pricked her breast, turning it eternally red. Damp acidic soils are vital for most low growing berries. Tastiest and juiciest are purplish black blaeberries (*Vaccinium myrtillus*) also called bilberries, whortleberries and whinberries, nestling in the heather with fruits often hidden beneath leaves that turn vivid

EXTRAORDINARY FACT

HARDER TO FIND

• Wild cranberry (*Vaccinium oxycoccus*): Once widespread, but now confined to the west and north, mainly due to the draining of bogs and marshes. Dark pink flowers borne on thin, wiry stems mature to white fruits that redded as they ripen.

• Crowberry (*Empetrum nigrum*): Fruit resembling bilberries but said to be fit for only corvids to eat. These small evergreens look like a pale green heather on the moors.

• Arctic bearberry (*Arctostaphylus alpinus*): Rare and almost always confined to the Highlands. Low mats of straggling stems bear toothed, dark green leaves turning bright red in autumn. Striking white flowers are followed by blackish purple berries.

orange in autumn. They are key foods for capercaillie, grouse and fieldfares as well as mice and deer, so should be harvested conservatively. Bearberries (*Arctostaphylos uva-ursi*), supposedly favoured by bears, have round, red holly like berries, in small groups amongst shiny, oval evergreen leaves. Although edible, they are best left to animals and birds. Similar, but growing in distinct clumps and with less shiny leaves, is the cowberry (*Vaccinium vitis-idaea*) with sharp marmalade tasting red fruit favoured by thrushes, blackbirds, squirrels and pine martens.

QUICK FACTS

- Being favourites of deer, wild raspberries are also called hindberries.

- In remote areas, blackberries mark the sites of abandoned settlements.

- Cowberry flowers are pollinated by bumblebees and hoverflies.

DID YOU KNOW?

Many wild berries have medical uses, and all are rich in vitamin C. Blaeberries, high in anthocyanins and polyphenols, are used to strengthen and protect the blood capillaries and to treat eyesight conditions. Raspberry leaf tea has long been valued for treating digestive and urinary problems, and to ease childbirth (but should never be taken in pregnancy). Bearberry leaf is a herbal remedy for urinary problems, while cowberry leaf is prized for its rich combination of protective antioxidants and anti-inflammatories. Cranberries are renowned for their ability to kill the bacteria causing urinary infections, but are only effective when highly concentrated.

Rasberries

COMMON, CONTROVERSIAL AND ANCIENT
Flourishing ferns

It unfurls its fronds in spring like bishops' crooks, flourishes in green swathes of green all summer, then in autumn turns to brilliant orange and brown. This is bracken (*Pteridium aquilinum*), most abundant of all wild ferns, whose ancestors are at least 55 million years old. Hardy up to 600 m (2,000 ft) it grows in woodlands, heathlands and grasslands and is especially prolific on south facing slopes and any situation providing the water and humidity on which it thrives. Firmly rooted by a network of rhizomes, new plants can grow and spread rapidly, and like other ferns it also reproduces via millions of microscopic spores contained in

THEN AND NOW
Traditionally bracken was essential – as bedding for both humans and animals, for making clamps to store root vegetables over the winter, for thatch and, from its high potassium content, for making soap, shampoo and even glass. Scots believed it was the Devil's footprint, a gateway to the underworld, home of fairies who could fall in love with young girls and sing to lure them to their fates. Medicinally, bracken was once used to treat ailments from rheumatism to nausea, blood and bladder problems and gynaecological conditions. Today it is mixed with wool and comfrey to make peat free compost.

the brownish orange clusters of sori on the leaf undersides. But bracken is controversial. Certainly it provides a welcome habitat for wildlife, especially mixed with other species, but can rapidly overtake pasture and sheep grazing areas. Cutting, and trampling by cattle, are traditional methods of bracken control, although impossible in harsh mountainous terrain. Until banned in 2023, the herbicide Asulan (Asulox) was used to control it, a move unwelcomed by many farmers.

> **AMAZING FACT**
>
> **FROM THE DINOSAUR WORLD**
>
> Close relations of ferns, clubmosses evolved around 320 million years ago; their fossilized remains became coal. A few still survive in Scotland, notably the fir clubmoss (*Huperzia selago*) which looks like a miniature conifer. Horsetails, with rough segmented stems, date to around 200 million years ago. Most remarkable is *Equisetum telmateia* which can grow to 2 m (6 ft).

QUICK FACTS

- The fern is the badge of the Clan Chisholm, originally from the Borders.

- Ferns were once thought to provide protection from witches.

- Bracken isn't eaten by either sheep or rabbits.

- Cattle and horses can be poisoned by eating bracken.

- Horsetails contain much silica and were once used as scouring pads.

- After dying down in autumn moonworts may not reappear for several years.

- Skye is especially rich in horsetails.

Clubmoss

EXTRAORDINARY FACT

SOME SPECIAL FERNS

• Mountain bladder fern (Cystopteris montana): Grows in shady, rocky sites above 700 m (2,300 ft) and only in the Highlands. Young fronds are covered in a delicate fuzz (tomentum) making them look silvery white.

• Moonwort (Botrychium lunaria): Unmistakeable for its grape like bunches of green spore-containing structures at the bases of its many lobed leaves.

• Hart's tongue fern (Asplenium scolopendrium): The only native fern with undivided leaves. Widely used in making cosmetics and in medicines including cough medicines, digestive treatments and astringents.

• Filmy ferns: Minute; often mistaken for lichens or liverworts. Gems of the rainforest. Wilson's filmy fern (Hymenophyllum wilsonii), found in dense patches, has thin, translucent leaves up to 20 cm (8 in) long, with veins growing right to the tips. The Killarney fern (Vandenboschia speciosa) is larger but even rarer. It has been found on Skye but its locations are secret from the public.

Moonwort

SHADES OF PURPLE, PINK – AND LUCKY WHITE
All among the heather

There are few more magnificent sights or scents than swathes of heather that cover the countryside from midsummer into autumn. Long ago, when woodlands were extensive, heather grew only on mountains and near the coast, but today is spread over some 20,000 sq km (5 million acres) of nutrient poor, acid moorland, often underlaid with peat. Most dominant is honey-scented ling (*Calluna vulgaris*), its masses of small flowers spreading down tangled stems densely packed with tiny evergreen leaves and providing vital shelter, food and nesting sites for grouse and other birds,

Heather plants will live for 30 years plus, but their woodiness, and ability to create new growth, wanes with age. This is the rationale behind muirburn, the now legally prescribed and controlled burning of heather, once every 15-20 years, and only between 1 October and 15 April, its timing aimed to afford maximum protection to reptiles and moorland birds, including plovers, pipits and grouse. However, the practice remains controversial, particularly because of its damage to sphagnum moss, loss of peat formation, and threats to biodiversity.

for small mammals, adders and insects, and nourishment for deer. Historically it has a host of domestic uses, from fuel to roofing and bedding and for brushes, brooms and baskets. And it is beloved of pollinators, especially bees. Heather honey has a taste like no other. In drier areas are clumps of bell heather (*Erica cinerea*) with bright pink bell-shaped flowers. Wetter spots are favoured habitats of its close relation the cross-leaved heath (*E. tetralix*) whose tight packed groups of pale pink blooms top long, branched stems bearing distinctive grey-green leaves.

Heather

EXTRAORDINARY FACT

A DRINK OF LEGEND

Brewed for over 4,000 years heather ale, with its smooth, floral, herbal notes, is enjoying renewed popularity. The company Williams Bros has been guardian of the ancient Gaelic recipe for '*Leann Fraoch*' since 1988 and remains its sole producer. In a famous legend recounted in verse by Robert Louis Stevenson (1850-94) Scotland, then ruled by the Picts, was being attacked by the Irish. When only two Scots survive – the Pictish king and his son – the Irish king tortures them, demanding the recipe for heather ale on pain of death. Doubting his son's ability to withstand torture, the Pictish king does a deal: if his son is killed quickly he will divulge the recipe. When the son dies, the king reneges, throwing himself to death on the rocks of the Mull of Galloway, so keeping the recipe safe.

LUCKY HEATHER

A spring of white heather is a good luck symbol often added to wedding bouquets. According to Celtic legend Malvina, daughter of the 3rd century poet Ossian, was heartbroken when the warrior Oscar, her betrothed, was killed in battle. As a token of his love the dying Oscar sent her a messenger bearing a spray of heather, but as Malvina's tears fell on the flowers, they turned white. She was then heard to say: 'although it is the symbol of my sorrow, may the white heather bring good fortune to all who find it'. Other versions declare that white heather grows only on ground unstained by battle's blood, possibly from the victory in 1544 of Clan Ranald, whose men wore the sprigs in their bonnets, or to the fortunate escape of Ewan of Cluny, Chief of Clan MacPherson, who hid in a patch of white heather following the battle of Culloden in 1746. From her time in Balmoral, Queen Victoria was intrigued by white heather and took its lucky tradition to England. In the garden, heather of any colour is believed to attract fairies while burning heather with bracken in the grate is an old spell for bringing rain.

QUICK FACTS

- In tests heather honey has proved as effective as manuka in boosting immunity.

- Heather was traditionally made into poultices and ointments to treat pain and inflammation. Other heather based medicines were administered for coughs, digestive problems and even blindness.

- The name ling widely used for 'common' heather, comes from the Anglo-Saxon *lig* or 'fire' from its use as a fuel.

> **DID YOU KNOW?**
>
> Many moth caterpillars rely on young heather for food. Most common is the fluffy brown and yellow oak eggar moth, Britain's largest day flier, whose males make unmistakable sharp zig-zags. Others often visible in daylight are the emperor with giant eye spots on both pairs of wings; the grey and white common heath, whose males have large, feathery antennae; and the true lover's knot whose reddish brown wings bear marks like Celtic crosses.

Oak eggar moth

GLORIOUS OR NOT?
The tale of the red grouse

The Glorious Twelfth, an August date once highly anticipated by gourmets as the beginning of the grouse shooting (and eating) season, is still a key date in the sporting calendar that ends the life of many red grouse or willow ptarmigans (*Lagopus lagopus scoticus*), the 'king' of game birds. Unless violently disturbed – as by a dog – red grouse stay mutely still in the heather that is both their food and their protection, but exploding into flight above the moorland they issue ironic shrill 'go-back, go-back, go-back' calls, followed by 'chuckles'. Feathered in many shades of brown, marked with black barring and with white feather tips, their distinctive red 'eyebrows' are especially prominent in males which, like their black relatives, perform theatrical mating displays. The name *Lagopus*, meaning 'hare like' comes from their feathered, whiteish legs and feet.

A MATTER OF OPINION

Grouse shooting was so popular in the Victorian age, helped by the burgeoning of rail travel and the invention of the breech-loading shotgun, that in 1910, 3,157 grouse shoots took place in Scotland. Today, around 10 per cent of the countryside is managed for grouse shooting, an activity attracting ever greater scrutiny from conservation and animal welfare organizations, with calls for strict licencing. The arguments run.

• Against: Grouse are medicated to keep their numbers up, with chemicals put into grit which can be eaten by other creatures, and mountain hares are killed unnecessarily as alleged disease transmitters. Although it is illegal to kill raptors such as golden eagles, buzzards and hen harriers, predators including foxes, stoats, weasels, crows and ravens are inhumanely trapped.

• For: The grouse shooting season, only 16 weeks long, is vital to the economy. Managing the moorland for shooting has benefitted other birds, notably curlews but also golden plover, meadow pipit, black grouse, dunlin and hen harrier.

EXTRAORDINARY FACT

The history of Famous Grouse whisky began in 1800 when John Brown established his grocery in Perth. In 1824 his daughter Margaret, married Matthew Gloag, whose name superseded that of her father in 1835. By his death in 1860 the company, which focussed mainly on wines, was doing well, but only in 1896 did Matthew Gloag III produce the company's first blended Scotch, 'Brig O Perth'. 'The Grouse', destined to become 'The Famous Grouse' nine years later, was first sold in the same year, with a distinctive label created by Gloag's daughter Philippa.

QUICK FACTS

- Red grouse have 16 different calls.

- Names for the bird include moor pout, moorfowl, muirfowl, moorcock and heather cock.

- Victorians regularly made bangles, cufflinks and other jewellery from grouse feet, claws and feathers.

Red grouse

REAL OR IMAGINARY?
Cats of the countryside

Rich in small rodent prey, woodlands and some grasslands of the Highlands are home to the elusive Scottish wildcat (*Felis silvestris silvestris*), one of Britain's three most endangered mammals now probably numbering around 200 individuals. Larger and stockier than their domestic relatives, their coats are marked with thick, dark stripes devoid of white and their tails distinctively striped and bushy with blunt, black ends. Confusion – and pure species decline – arises from significant interbreeding with feral cats, which has created the large, handsome, almost pure black long-legged hybrid Kellas cat, named for the Moray village where it was first recorded in 1983.

★ AMAZING FACT ★

THE MYTHICAL FELINE
Described as all-black – but for the white spot on its chest – the *cat-sìth* that haunts the Highlands is said to steal the souls of the dead before their burial. To prevent this evil, it was once thought essential to keep watch over corpses at night, but on 1 November, the Gaelic feast of Samhain marking the start of winter, householders would leave a saucer of milk outside the door for the *cat-sìth* to be sure of receiving a blessing that would prevent their cows' milk from drying up.

> To comply with the law governing dangerous wild animals that may attack people and livestock it is essential to report any big cat sightings to the police.

QUICK FACTS

- The wildcat lifespan is 10 to 12 years.

- An adult female weighs around 4 kg (9 lb), a male 5 kg (11 lb).

- Females give birth to litters of 2 to 6 kittens, usually in May, and are weaned for 5 months.

- The best time to spot wildcats is between dusk and dawn.

EXTRAORDINARY FACT

Over the years hundreds of 'big cats' have been recorded in Scotland, most commonly in Highland, Aberdeenshire, Fife and Moray. Many are linked with the death of sheep, their carcasses stripped by attacks impossible to attribute to foxes, dogs or birds. Typical descriptions are of creatures as big as large dogs but with panther like features. Mauled calves with tails ripped off are also thought to be big cat victims. Since 2000 there have been continuous reports of a big cat roaming woodland around Edzell in Angus while Aberdeenshire's famous Beast of Bennachie was seen regularly during the 1990s.

Scottish wildcat

FOR PEAT'S SAKE
Precious carbon stores

For a warming world it is black gold. Almost a fifth of Scotland is covered with peat – dead plants such as sphagnum moss that do not decay fully as they die but, over centuries, build up layers of carbon rich peat. And because peat accumulates at only 1 mm a year, it is even more precious. Scotland's peatland stores 25 times more carbon than other types of vegetation and when in good condition keeps its essential wet, acidic, low oxygen conditions maintained. But if peatlands begin to dry out they quickly start releasing carbon dioxide and methane, contributing to global warming. Traditionally, peat was a vital fuel for families, who cut it into blocks and let it dry, selling it also in local towns. Draining peatlands and heavy grazing by animals are also destructive, but much work is currently being done to restore bare areas and halt erosion. Equally, intensive peat harvesting for garden composts is beginning to diminish.

Butterwort

★ AMAZING FACT ★

PRETTY BUT DEADLY

Obvious for their bright purple flowers, it is the yellow-green leaves of butterworts (*Pinguicula* spp) that are most extraordinary, secreting a sticky fluid that attracts insect food. Once trapped the leaves curl around then digest them with an array of enzymes. Its scientific name means 'little greasy one'. By Scottish tradition, butterworts were hung over house doors when a corpse within was awaiting burial. Because it was also believed to be able to protect milk from being 'turned' or curdled by witches, leaves were rubbed on cows' udders for protection.

EXTRAORDINARY FACT

Walking on it feels like treading on a soft sponge – hardly surprising as sphagnum moss can hold 30 times its own weight in water. Scotland has 34 species in a variety of colours and textures, each favouring a subtly different habitat, but three are particularly key to the peatlands. Pale green Sphagnum cuspidatum is the 'drowned kitten' moss of pools, looking like bunches of green fur. S. capillifolium, the red bog moss, is a striking pinkish maroon, forming sizeable clumps, while the yellow green S. papillosum has typically short, spreading branches. Since the 1950s, huge quantities of sphagnum have been removed by the gardening business, but it has many historical uses. Acting like a sponge (it has no roots), it is an ancient wound dressing notably valued in WWI. Its biochemical ability to create an environment hostile to bacteria has now been scientifically proven.

The lowlands have bogs too. Here they are raised domes of peat topped with mounds of sphagnum, sedges and, as farther north, carnivorous sundews (Drosera spp). In May and June carpets of white cotton buds – the heads of cotton or ghost grass (Eriophorum angustifolium), a sedge that is neither cotton nor grass – sway in the breeze, its leaves providing vital food for the caterpillars of endangered large heath butterflies. Emperor moths, dragonflies and damselflies enliven the air here too. Much rarer, living at the bases of grassy tussocks are the sun-jumping spiders, distinguished by their iridescent green mouthparts, found in only five sites in central Scotland.

BLANKET BOG

Caithness and Sutherland are home to the Flow Country, peatland and wetland containing Europe's largest expanse of blanket bog – peatland criss-crossed with dark water courses occasionally forming 'mini lochs'. Containing 8,000 years of natural history, blanket bog is created only where it is cool and wet. Here, mosses and other plants decay, gradually forming layers of peat that can be 10 m (33 ft) thick (the height of two double decker buses) and storing three times more carbon that all of Britain's woodlands. As well as mosses, sundews and butterworts, carnivorous plants that rely for life on catching and digesting insects (especially midges) in these low oxygen conditions are abundant. Here birds including golden plovers, dunlin and greenshank thrive along with scoters and black-throated divers. Overhead hen harriers and merlin search for shrews and unwary chicks. Breeding conditions are ideal for frogs,

Golden plover

toads, newts and lizards, and on warm days adders emerge to bask in the sun. Now protected, the blanket bogs were threatened in in 1970s and 80s when non-native trees were introduced, sucking up vital water, but the schemes were stopped in time to avoid lasting damage; repair programmes continue today.

QUICK FACTS

- A bucket and a half of peat contains about 1 kg (2 lb) of carbon.

- The carbon locked in Scotland's peatlands is equal to 140 years of the country's total greenhouse gas emissions.

- Sphagnum reproduces from spores released from shiny black capsules and can travel long distances on the air.

- Glossy great diving beetles live in shallow peaty bog waters.

- Most of the UK's 50 breeding pairs of common scoters are found in Scotland's blanket bogs.

- Peatlands' crane flies are a key food for red grouse and other birds.

- Prehistoric burial chambers have been discovered in the Flow Country.

- Cotton grass is a key food for black grouse.

- Avoid cotton grass areas when walking – they almost aways have their roots in water.

APPROACH WITH CAUTION
Plants with extraordinary powers

Although beautiful, some plants have fearsome reputations. Its showers of white flowers, borne on bare branches make the blackthorn (*Prunus spinosa*) spring's harbinger but is believed to grow from heathens' corpses. Cursed and unlucky, it is the Devil's possession, used to mark and identify witches' skins. The witches, in turn, used it to prick wax images of their victims. But sloes (blackthorn berries) have protective powers. In legend blackthorn embodies Beira, the Queen of Winter, her head covered with a blue veil. With a raven on her shoulder, a wave of her blackthorn staff would command storms. Hawthorn (*Crataegus monogyna*), is lucky unless brought indoors when

Hawthorn

EXTRAORDINARY FACT

Protection is afforded by the rowan or mountain ash (*Sorbus aucuparia*) and the elder (*Sambucus nigra*). The rowan, the 'Lady of the mountain', 'quicken tree' or 'wildwood', protects humans and animals from witches, evil spirits and disasters of all kinds. Significantly, the five-pointed star on each fruit resembles the magical pentagram. The rowan or 'whispering tree' is also a keeper of secrets when the wind rustles its leaves. The elder is guarded by the benign Mother Elder; before flowers or berries are harvested her permission must be sought with a gentle touch. And an elder wand gives Harry Potter his power.

in flower, having the odour of the plague. Its branches were used as divining rods. In the 13th century, after lying under a hawthorn at Earlston in the Borders, one Thomas Rhymer is believed to have been taken to a magical world by the Fairy Queen. On returning he had acquired a gift of prophesy.

ABOUT THE YEWS
Yews (**Taxus baccata**) *are graveyards' conifers, planted to protect the departed and symbolize life after death long before churches were built alongside. In a churchyard west of Aberfeldy is the famous Fortingall Yew, certainly over 3,000 (and possibly as much as 9,000) years old. Even when first recorded in writing in 1769 its trunk measured a massive 16 m (52 ft) in girth. Believed to be one of the oldest living things in Europe, funeral processions still pass under the arch of its branches although the trunk is now split into several different parts. Legend has it that Pontius Pilate played in it as a child. In Shakespeare's* **Macbeth** *'slips of yew, silvered in the moon's eclipse' are ingredients of the witches' brew. Yew wood is ideal for longbows; those commissioned by Robert the Bruce (1274-1329) from the sacred yews at Ardchattan Priory in Argyll aided his victory at Bannockburn in 1314.*

QUICK FACTS
• Cuttings grown from the Fortingall Yew now form a hedge in Edinburgh's Royal Botanic Gardens. The area around it contains Bronze Age archaeological sites.

• In Scotland the rowan grows at higher altitudes than any other tree.

• A sprig of yew is the badge of Clan Fraser.

• Yews are the source anti-cancer drugs.

DID YOU KNOW?

Junipers (*Juniperus communis*) are believed to be gossips, so secrets should never be shared near them. Now in decline, over 80 per cent of wild trees in the UK grow in Scotland which are in two forms, upright and prostrate (dwarf or low growing). The 'berries' (actually small cones), used to flavour whisky in Medieval times, are now mostly added to gin; they were once used to dispel unwanted pregnancies.

Juniper

THE HEIGHT OF BEAUTY
Scotland's alpine flora

If they are to survive, the flowers of the highest peaks must emerge, grow and flower, then and set and release seed, in just four months. Through the rest of the year these perennials lie dormant in freezing soil, battered by wind and snow. Of all the places to see these arctic beauties in their greatest variety, many of them endangered, best is the Ben Lawers nature reserve in Perthshire. Here, shining in brilliant blue, are alpine gentians (*Gentiana nivalis*) and forget-me-nots (*Myosotis alpestris*), contrasting with the yellow flowered

Bog asphodel

The specific name of the bog asphodel (*Narthecium ossifragum*), common in the mountains, translates literally as 'bone breaker' as it was thought that livestock grazing on it developed brittle bones, a condition actually caused by calcium poor pastures. In mythology asphodels are linked with death and the underworld.

EXTRAORDINARY FACT

SPECIAL WILLOWS

Although vulnerable to grazing by deer and sheep, and increasingly lacking protective snow cover, at Ben Lawers rare mountain willows are being re-established, many of them growing on bare ledges, including:

• Net-leaved or snow willow (*Salix reticulata*): Named for the net like pattern of veins on its low growing leaves. Produces pink catkins in spring on dark red twigs.

• Woolly willow (*S. lantana*): Rare in Britain; leaves are covered with a dense coat of white hairs which, as in animals, helps heat retention. The catkins are a silvery pale yellow.

• Downy willow (*S. lapponum*): Leaves are also hairy but much smaller and thinner. Catkins are a silky grey.

Snow willow

alpine cinquefoils (*Potentilla crantzii*) and rock lady's mantles (*Alchemilla wichurae*). Lying close to the ground for protection from the wind, like many of its neighbours, is the pink flowered trailing azalea (*Kalmia procumbens*) while in bright white are the flowers of mountain avens (*Dryas octopelata*) which, like sunflowers, follow the sun as it moves across the sky each day.

> **QUICK FACTS**
> • As well as flowers, Ben Lawers is an important location for mosses and liverworts including the rare moss *Roaldia revoluta*.
>
> • The snake-like Newman's lady fern (A*thyrium flexile*) is found nowhere in the world but Scotland, at an altitude of at least 750 m (2,460 ft).

TUMBLING CASCADES
The wonders of waterfalls

Crashing and thundering through gorges and rippling down often remote mountainsides, Scotland's majestic waterfalls have inspired poets, writers and artists, and many myths and legends. As ice melted and retreated from Scotland 10,000 years ago, gashes where water now cascades were slowly carved into the landscape as the rocks below were worn away. Among the highest, with a drop of around 60 m (197 ft) the Falls of Bruar near Pitlochry in Perth and Inverness, were the inspiration for 'The Humble Petition of Bruar Water to the Noble Duke of Atholl', Robert Burns' poem in which he pleads for 'tow'ring trees' and 'bonnie spreading bushes' to be planted

Cascade at the Aray at Inveraray

> **QUICK FACTS**
>
> • Visiting waterfalls was a favoured Victorian leisure pursuit.
>
> • Loch Skeen is home to Britain's rarest freshwater fish, the vendace (*Coregonus albula*).

in the bare landscape. Ten years later Burns (1759-96) began a scheme that eventually included 120,000 trees, mainly larch and Scots pine. More emotive still are the remote 15m (50 ft) Wailing Widow Falls on Skye, named from the legend of a mother who came to weep after her son's untimely end here. At any waterfall a *caoineag*, a Highland banshee, might foretell the death of a clan member by crying out at night.

> **EXTRAORDINARY FACT**
>
> With a sheer cascade of 194 m (638 ft), and in full flow over three times the height of Niagara Falls, Eas a'Chual Aluinn, in Sutherland plunges into Loch Beag. Its name, meaning 'waterfall of the beautiful tresses' comes from its likeness to a woman's flowing hair. While visible from the water, the top of the falls is reachable only on foot on a steep path traversing boggy and steep rocky ground. From the glassy waters of Loch Skeen in Dumfries and Galloway, the aptly named Grey Mare's Tail is a plunges 60 m (197 ft) into Moffat Water below. Not only a superb example of a hanging valley (a small 'side valley' left isolated above a main U-shaped valley as a glacier retreated) it is a haven for peregrine falcons, ospreys and ring ouzels and rare plants including the oblong woodsia, montane willows, and alpine saw-wort. Fossil hunters can find graptolites here and there is more recent evidence of Iron Age settlements.

MAGNIFICENT WATER
- Den Finella Waterfall, Aberdeenshire: The 'lost' waterfall of Scotland named from a noblewoman said to have leapt to her death here. She had sought to kill king Kenneth II (932-95) after he had killed her son.
- Plodda Falls, Invergordon: Water plunging 46 m (151 ft) through pine forests can be viewed from a visitor platform.
- Falls of Dochart, Perthshire: After crashing down the rocks water rushes around the island of Inchbuie, ancient burial place of the clan MacNab.
- Falls of Measach, Highlands: Named 'waterfalls of the place of platters' from the many holes created by swirling water; 46 m (151 ft) high.

SPIRITS OF THE WATER
The legendary kelpies

Able to shape shift between humans and black or grey horses, kelpies reside in Scotland's rivers, streams and lochs. Often hairy in human form, and endowed with hooves pointing in reverse, as they enter the water their tails make sounds like thunder. It is said that kelpies can predict the demise of those in their power and, accompanied by flashing lights and loud noise, can even assist in their drowning, taking

> **QUICK FACTS**
>
> - When resident in or beside a loch a kelpie is called an *each-uisge*.
>
> - One kelpie is said to have the strength of 100 horses.
>
> - Kelpies are traditionally male but at Conan House in Ross and Cromarty is described as a tall, scowling woman dressed in green with a malign and meagre countenance.
>
> - Robert Burns refers to kelpies and their association with Satan in his 1786 poem 'Address to the Devil'.

them to the water's edge, killing and eating them before throwing their remains into the water. Kelpie tales abound, as at Loch Pityoulish, near Aviemore, where nine children, attracted by a 'pretty pony', are believed to have been lured to a watery death by a kelpie. In Shetland the Njuggles have similar forms, favouring children as their victims.

Kelpies at Helix Park, Falkirk

DID YOU KNOW?

Helix Park, between Falkirk and Grangemouth, is home to dramatic Kelpies, horses' heads created by Andy Scott (b.1964) in 2013. Originally conceived as mythological creatures whose transforming powers reflect the changes in the landscape, they celebrate overtly the history of horses in industry and agriculture. The pair are modelled on Duke and Baron, two historical Clydesdale horses that once pulled ploughs, wagons and barges. Each standing 30 m (98 ft) tall, they are in structural steel with a stainless steel cladding but hollow, allowing visitors to enter.

EXTRAORDINARY FACT

At Loch Garve in the Highlands a kelpie lived with his unhappy, shivering wife in the deepest, coldest waters. So he propelled himself to the surface, became a handsome horse and travelled to a builder's home. Sensing his mission, the builder climbed onto the kelpie's back, then was shocked as he entered the water. Now he discovered his task – to build a warm home for the wife fitted with a fireplace and chimney to take smoke to the surface. His reward? A limitless supply of fish. Today, even when Loch Garve freezes over there is always an ice-free spot, thanks to the unquenchable fire below.

A TRIUMPH OF CONSERVATION
The osprey's successful return

Resident in Scotland since the end of the last ice age, by 1916 ospreys or fish hawks (*Pandion haliaeetus*) had been wiped out. The hunters of these magnificent birds were Victorian trophy seekers wanting to display stuffed birds in their cabinets but also, because ospreys feed solely on fish, notably salmon and trout, were pursued to their deaths by commercial fisheries. In 1954, a solitary pair began breeding again high in a tree of a long-abandoned site near Loch Garten, but remained threatened by egg collectors even when in 1958, despite 24-hour vigils by volunteers, eggs were stolen and smashed. The following year, with the help of wooden walkways (for swift intervention) and phone lines, Operation Osprey began; the ospreys, however, settled on a brand new nest site

Osprey

EXTRAORDINARY FACT

As it dives for fish – it is not fussy about species – an osprey can hit the water at over 48 km/h (30 mph). As they enter the water their fleshy nostrils close up and their eyelids are protected by sliding transparent membranes. Prey are caught using specialized feet like those of an owl, topped with razor sharp claws; they have reversible outer toes, providing a fierce grip as they push against the rear ones. A hooked beak is ideal for tearing flesh. To lift off carrying up to 500g (17 oz) of squirming fish ospreys rely on their powerful wingbeats. Nesting begins each year in spring when birds return some 6,500 km (4,000 miles) from west Africa, ardent males often bringing so many sticks that the females are almost buried. The chicks fledge and mature from July to September.

on the opposite side of the loch. Stealthy by night, the defences were quickly moved and three chicks successfully fledged. Despite the efforts of vandals, ospreys now number around 300 breeding pairs in Scotland, many continuing to use ancestral nests hundreds of years old, others inhabiting artificial nesting platforms.

QUICK FACTS

- The osprey has a large head, feathered in white and distinctive brown eye stripes. The back is brown and the underbelly a brownish black.

- When migrating they can cover 645 km (400 miles) in a day.

- King James I is said to have kept ospreys and trained them to fish.

- Ospreys were believed to have magical powers drawing fish to them.

Critical to saving the osprey were George Waterson, then Scotland's head of the RSPB, and his decision to allow the public to observe annual osprey breeding at Loch Garten. Over 14,000 visitors came initially, the total now exceeds two million. Loch Lomond, Loch Ruthven and the river Glass are other great locations for seeing ospreys in action.

RARE AND RARER
Water wildlife, present and future

Until the 16th century, when hunted to extinction, beavers (*Castor fiber*) were common Scottish residents only reintroduced in 2009, initially to what is now Beaver Trail at Knapdale, Argyll and in parts of the river Tay. From 2023 they arrived in the Loch Lomond Nature Reserve. These industrious,

> **QUICK FACTS**
>
> - There are plans to introduce beavers to the Cairngorms.
>
> - Beavers do not hibernate. They live in family groups of three to five.
>
> - Compared with otters, beavers swim much higher in the water.
>
> - Around 40 per cent of Britain's water voles live in Scotland, mostly in the Highlands.
>
> - Pearl mussels have been estimated to live well over 100 years.

amphibious creatures, intensely muscled and as large as Labrador dogs, have short legs, webbed feet and broad, flat, scaly tails. By felling trees and bushes to create dams, beavers are key players in the ecosystem. By slowing water flow (dams leak continuously) they collect pollutants and sediments, so minimizing flooding. Where they 'coppice' trees by removing branches, new growth quickly sprouts, creating protective habitats for small mammals and insects. A dam broken by a storm can be repaired within days. Within 'beaver meadows', endangered water voles (*Arvicola amphibius*), find welcome protection, although still vulnerable to attack by mink. With dark brown, almost black fur they are excellent swimmers and can be seen carrying nesting materials in their mouths. Uniquely shaped greenish brown droppings (like Tic-Tacs) on banksides are a sure sign of their presence.

EXTRAORDINARY FACT

PRECIOUS MOLLUSCS

Appreciated since Roman times, and now legally protected, freshwater pearl mussels (*Margaritifera margaritifera*), have long lived in Scottish rivers but in 2023 were discovered in lochs in Sutherland and the Trossachs, probably transported clinging to fishes' gills. Early in their life cycle the mussels live harmlessly on young salmon and trout, before dropping off to live on riverbeds. With mother of pearl shell linings, they can also create true pearls.

Beavers were hunted for their dense fur measuring 230,000 hairs/sq cm (365,000/sq in) and for castoreum, a yellowish secretion used to mark their territories. This was prized for perfumery (it smells like leather), made into a tincture with alcohol and even dried, crushed and added to food.

BESIDE STILL WATERS
Exploring freshwater lochs

From the celebrated Lomond and Ness, Scotland boasts some 27,000 freshwater lochs. As glaciation ended and ice retreated, they formed the U-shaped valleys enclosing larger lochs but in some places blocks of 'dead' ice were left behind. Here they became encased in sediment and, when they finally melted, left smaller lochs in kettle holes such as Loch Morlich in the Cairngorms, surrounded by snow-capped mountains for much of the year, and Loch Fergus in Ayrshire farmland. Stormont Loch in Perthshire, fringed with peaty fen, hence its alternative name of Loch Bog, is scientifically renowned. Because it has remained undisturbed, the changes in its vegetation over the last 13,000 years have been recorded in detail. Where blanket bog prevails, small, shallow dubh lochans are common, their water stained yellow or brown.

EXTRAORDINARY FACT

WATER WILDLIFE

- The yellow water lily (N*uphar lutea*) graces many lochs where it can bury its roots in silt and is known as the brandy bottle from the shape and scent of its seed heads. Where nutrients are low bogbean (M*enyanthes trifoliata*) with starry white flowers can flourish along with carnivorous, yellow-flowered bladderworts (U*tricularia vulgaris*) which trap and digest water fleas and other small invertebrates.

- Water voles, among Scotland's most threatened species, burrow in loch sides. Except in the far north they remain threatened by mink. Otters also thrive in healthy waters.

- Black throated divers and Slavonian grebes are rarer loch residents.

- The biggest threat to lochs is the presence of pollutants, including pesticides used in fish farms. Pollution increases the growth of algae and the growth of invasive plants including the New Zealand pygmy weed, water fern and both Canadian and Nuttall's pondweed.

QUICK FACTS

- At 71 sq km (27.4 sq miles) Loch Lomond has the largest surface area.
- Loch Ness is the largest by volume containing 7,452 million cubic metres (263,000 cubic ft) of water.
- Deepest is Loch Morar at 310 m (1,017 ft).
- Longest end to end is Loch Awe at 40 km (25 miles).
- Scotland's most photographed tree the lone oak, anchored with twisted roots, rises from the water at Milarrochy Bay on Loch Lomond's eastern shore.

AMONG THE BEST

- Loch Affric, Highlands: Surrounded by ancient pinewoods and moorland. Perfect for spotting golden eagles, ospreys, red deer, red squirrels and even crossbills and wildcats. Good for trout fishing.
- Loch Muick (pronounced 'Mick'), Aberdeenshire: Within the Balmoral Estate and beloved of Queen Victoria. The nearby mountain Lochnagar is a lifelong favourite of King Charles III.
- Loch Morar, Highland: The deepest loch and also the home of a 'monster'. Largely inaccessible to cars but surrounded by mixed evergreen and deciduous woodland.
- Loch Tay, Perthshire: Site of ancient dwellings of Beaker people from the Bronze Age and Iron Age crannogs. Overlooked on the north shore by Ben Lawers, home to many raptors and other birds, plus the threatened white flowered alpine the mountain sandwort (*Sabulina rubella*).
- Loch Awe, Argyll: At 40 km (25 miles) long, Scotland's longest loch and a world famous salmon fishing destination.
- Loch Katrine, Stirlingshire: The tranquil inspiration for Sir Walter Scott's poem *The Lady of the Lake* and home to its romantic wooded islet Ellen's Isle. Its name derives from the Gaelic *cateran*, or 'highland robber'. Most notable of these was Rob Roy Macgregor, born at Glengyle House at the northern end.
- Loch Skeen, Dumfries and Galloway: Renowned for its peregrine falcons and the Grey Mare's Tail waterfall. Only accessible on foot but rewarding for its moorlands and graptolite fossils, the remains of ocean dwelling colonial filter feeders that look like ferny outlines on the rocks.

⋆ AMAZING FACT ⋆

IN BRIGHT COLOUR
Green Loch in the Cairngorms, renowned for its vivid deep turquoise water, is said to have been coloured when pixies or fairies washed their clothes. In fact the hues come partly from algae and partly from reflections of lochside trees. Called *An Lochan Uaine* in Gaelic it sits below a mountain named Angel's Peak. The water is icy cold – and home to leeches.

THE BONNIE, BONNIE BANKS

The famous song that celebrates Loch Lomond praises its beauty, but essentially relates the tragedy of two Scottish brothers imprisoned in England's Carlisle Castle following the battle of Culloden, one to be freed, the other condemned to execution. The younger brother chooses to give up his life so his older brother can live, taking the 'low road', route for the souls of the dead, while the elder brother not only lives but takes the 'high road' back to the moors and mountains of home. Surrounded by hills, including Ben Lomond, the loch contains some 30 islands including Inchmurrin the largest freshwater island in the British Isles. Some of the islands, known as crannogs, are artificial; they were built from the Bronze Age onwards as protection from marauders, both human and animal. Discovered on the eastern shore in 1936 the Scottish *dock (***Rumex aquaticus***) is unique to Britain. Of all lochs, Lomond's waters support the most fish including lamprey, perch, brown trout, roach and flounder. Recent arrivals are the beavers introduced in 2023; the red-necked wallabies first brought in the 1940s still survive on Inchconnachan.*

DEEP, DARK AND MYSTERIOUS
The legendary Loch Ness

When, according to legend Nessa, maid to the Celtic winter queen Dark Beira or Cailleach Bheur, was late attending to her duties the queen turned her into a river. Not only did she escape but she stretched and stretched to become Loch Ness, home of the elusive monster. Geologically, the forces that formed the loch began when around 430 to 390 million years ago a massive fault – the Great Glen – opened up between Fort William and Inverness as rocks slid past each other. Millennia later, today's loch – the UK's largest body of water – was established as the final glaciers retreated 10,000 years ago. Black with peat washed from surrounding hills, light penetrates to only 9 m (30 ft), enhancing monster mysteries. It is cold, but never freezes over. The deeper waters, at their

★ AMAZING FACT ★

A WAY IN
Because Loch Ness is connected via the Caledonian Canal to Beauly Firth on the east coast, seals, porpoises and bottlenose dolphins can enter by surviving treacherous journeys up the river Ness. But being marine dwellers they can only live around 48 hours in freshwater. Resident fish include salmon, pike and eel, but most fearsome is the ferox trout, a massive brown trout that may even turn cannibal, behaviour that evolved in the nutrient poor water devoid of insects and other small invertebrates.

maximum 247 m (812 ft), remain at 5.5°C all year round, those at the surface average 4.6°C in winter but 15.1°C in summer. The release of chemicals into the loch encourages the growth of algae, including the blue-green species that can harm human health. This, and the risk of hypothermia, make swimming unadvisable.

Ferox trout

EXTRAORDINARY FACT

TRICKSTERS' TALES
Among alleged monster sightings are some notable hoaxes. In the early 1970s the ornithologist Peter Scott named it N*essiteras rhombopteryx* after seeing a blurred underwater photograph taken by the American lawyer Robert Rines. The name is an anagram of 'monster hoax by Sir Peter S'. In 1994 it came to light that one Marmaduke Wetherall had faked a famous photograph of a long-necked creature attributed to surgeon RK Wilson in 1934. On 2 July 2003 a Mr Gerald McSorley reported discovering bones on the shore but on expert analysis were identified as plesiosaur vertebrae encased in a limestone never found at the loch.

THE NESSIE MYSTERY
Monster of the loch

In 565 CE, so St Adomnan's *Life of St Columba* recorded, the saint raised his voice to a creature in Loch Ness, so saving the life of a swimmer being attacked by a 'water beast'. Centuries later, on 2 May 1933, the *Inverness Courier* told the story of 'an enormous animal', which the editor dubber 'a monster' seen 'rolling and plunging' by Mr and Mrs John Mackay. A media frenzy ensued and on 13 November that year Hugh Gray used his Kodak Box Brownie to snap a 'humped creature' (now thought to have been a dog). Regular 'Nessie' stories have followed ever since, and also scientific exploration. In 1981 the Loch Ness Project led by naturalist Adrian Shine built a sonar research vessel to make systematic patrols. Strong echoes were recorded, as they were in a 1987 operation, some of which could have been the release of methane gas from decaying vegetation. Significantly this research discovered huge underwater waves created as surface winds move layers of water – plus logs and other floating objects – against the prevailing wind. In 2023 hundreds joined a two-day monster hunt but with no results of note.

> **QUICK FACTS**
> - The Great Glen is 100 km (62 miles) long.
> - There is more water in Loch Ness than all the lakes in England and Wales combined.
> - The Monster has appeared in many fictional contexts from The Simpsons to Dr Who, Blue Peter and the 1970 film *The Private Life of Sherlock Holmes*.
> - In 1933 a circus offered a reward of £20,000 for a captured monster.
> - The Loch Ness Project is a reference site for scientific exploration and the monster controversy.
> - By 2024 official sitings had exceeded 1,141.

Bluebell

On the loch's south shore are the remnants of an ancient forest whose trees include the downy birch (*Betula pubescens*), a pioneer species that established itself after the ice retreated. Here bluebells carpet the woodland floor in spring accompanied by mountain pansies. In autumn emerge a variety of fungi, among them the edible chicken of the woods, cep and hedgehog fungus and the brilliant purple amethyst deceiver.

NOT JUST NESSIE
Creatures of the lochs

Loch Ness is not the only monster venue. From the 1887 century there have been sightings of the 'dark humps like upturned boats' of the monster Morag alternately appearing and disappearing in the deep waters

AMAZING FACT

POOLS OF MAGIC
Ringed by the dark, foreboding Cuillin Hills, the clear turquoise waters of Skye's Fairy Pools, fed ceaselessly by small waterfalls, are believed to be home to selkies, mythical creatures that swim as seals during the day but shed their skins and bathe as humans at night. Here, too, the local chief of Clan MacLeod is said to have married a fairy princess.

of Loch Morar. Morag, long necked and covered with reptilian skin, is said to have all but capsized fishing boats and even left her footprints on shore. In one incident two local men Duncan McDonell and William Simpson described a rough-skinned brown creature around 8 m (27 ft) long with three humps and a head about 30 cm (1 ft) wide which, after being threatened with McDonell's oar, sank back into the depths. But documents dating to 1902 written by Alexander Carmichael (1832-1912) describe a timid creature like a mermaid with large breasts and long flowing blonde hair said to be visible only immediately before a death, particularly a drowning.

QUICK FACTS

- Some say that Nessie and Morag are related and that their lochs 112.5 km (70 miles) apart connected by a yet undiscovered water-filled tunnel.

- In 1961 hoaxers planted and photographed an artificial monster in Loch Oich.

- Loch Mallachie is known as the Loch of the Curse.

- *Bodach* is a general term for a bogeyman or trickster as well as a phantom. It appears in many Scottish place names such as Bodach Mòr and Bodach Beag in the Highlands.

EXTRAORDINARY FACT

On 13 August 1936 Alderman AJ Richards was boating with his son on Loch Oich when a near-black creature loomed from the water nearby. He told of a double humped snake-like monster with a head like a dog. The humps, he reported, were about 1 m (3 ft) high and the same distance apart. An earlier, bizarre story told of the monster killing a child who drowned after climbing onto its back onshore before being hurled into the water.

> **DID YOU KNOW?**
>
> Both Loch Garten and Loch Mallachie are said to be inhabited by a *Bodach* or spirit, a huge white phantom that roams at night emitting high pitched screams warning anyone she met of an imminent, violent death. Such weird groaning noises are actually made by air escaping from ice as it melts in spring. Loch Morlich in the Cairngorms is believed to be home, on its west side, to the King of the Fairies, while on east side dwells the Spectre of the Bloody Hand, guardian of animals and an old man dressed as a Highland warrior who, using his hand dripping with blood, will massacre anyone he meets. Appearing alongside lochs (and also waterfalls) the *Caoineag* is a weeping spirit woman whose appearance signifies death.

MASTERS OF THE WATER
The life of otters

Otter

Five-toed footprints in waterside mud, and prominent spraint (droppings) packed with fish bones and mollusc shells and smelling sweetly of hay or jasmine tea, are the tell-tale signs of otters (*Lutra lutra*) or 'dratsies'. By the water, watch for long chains of bubbles created as they slowly breathe out and for the V-shaped wakes of their lithe bodies as they swim, using webbed feet and muscular, rudder-like tails. Of Scotland's 8,000 otters, most visible at dawn and dusk, around half live away from the shore but all are protected, including their holts (homes). From the top of the aquatic food chain, otters consume up to 1.5 kg (3.3 lb) of prey daily, including trout, salmon and eels but also frogs, toads and even small birds.

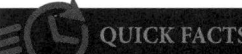

QUICK FACTS
- Otters deposit their spraint in prominent places such as on fallen trees and bridges to mark their territories and to attract mates.

- The long, sensitive whiskers are vital for detecting prey.

EXTRAORDINARY FACT

OTTERS IN LEGEND
According to myth, otter kings are accompanied by seven black otters. If captured, they will readily grant any wish to secure their freedom. An otter king could only be killed by striking it directly on a small black spot beneath its chin. Ancient legend relates that Eilean Donan, an island in Loch Duich in the western Highlands, is the burial place of one such silver coated king. Whoever finds his coat will be rewarded with immortality and invincibility. In Loch Ness, families of otters swimming in line and leaping to catch fish are regularly misidentified as the Monster.

While the use of pesticides resulted in otters virtually disappearing from England and Wales in the mid 20th century, Scottish populations fared much better. The ancient sport of otter hunting with hounds, which made the wearing of otter skin waistcoats a fashion in some parts, was banned in Scotland in 1982.

LEAPING FOR THEIR LIVES
Salmon and their journeys

The silvery glint of an Atlantic salmon (*Salmo salar*) leaping some 4 m (13 ft) from the rushing waters of a Highland river is an awesome sight – and becoming ever rarer. Now this 'king of fish', still eager to reach its birthplace, will fall back into the torrent, before leaping again. It may be successful but many fail, even if aided by ladders. After hatching from one of thousands of fertilized eggs released by their mothers and around 2 cm (less than 1 in) long, alevins feed on eggs' yolk sacs, emerging by six weeks as fry. For the next months (now known as parr), and even for as long as three years, they feed voraciously, but will be lucky to escape the jaws of herons, otters and other predators. With juvenile stripes now replaced by silvery scales they swim as smolts to the ocean. Within six years they will head for home where, on arrival, they will mate, then die exhausted.

> **AMAZING FACT**
>
> **A RECORD CATCH**
> On 7 October 1922 Georgina Ballantine made history by landing a 29 kg (64 lb) salmon from the river Tay with the help of her ghillie. It took two hours to land and remains one of the longest standing records in the UK. Apart from December, salmon fishing can be enjoyed in Scotland all year. That it takes place mainly on private estates limits the number of fish that can be caught.

Salmon

DID YOU KNOW?

Early morning and evening from July to November, especially after heavy rain, are the best times to see leaping salmon. Among the prime locations are:
- The Lin of Tummel near Pitlochry; has a ladder built in 1910.
- The bridge at Rogie Falls on the Black Water river, Ross-shire.
- The Falls of the Braan, Dunkeld, in the Hermitage.
- Sites along the river Dee, notably Mar Lodge, Braemar.

QUICK FACTS

- Wild salmon were internationally classified as endangered in 2023.
- The salmon's name probably comes from the Latin *salire*, meaning 'to leap'.
- Since it was built in 1952 the ladder at Pitlochry has been crossed by over 250,000 salmon.
- Salmon's healthy ingredients, including omega 3 fatty acids, are indeed good for the brain.
- The Celtic salmon symbol of Clan Donald is one of the oldest of its kind, dated to at least 125 BCE.

EXTRAORDINARY FACT

In folklore the salmon is a source of knowledge and wisdom and an ancient Celtic symbol still seen in the Glasgow coat of arms and on pub signs. Legend has it that Queen Languoreth of Strathclyde was accused by her husband, King Rhydderch, of gifting a ring he had given her before their marriage to her lover. In fact, he had taken it from his rival's finger whilst he slept and thrown it into the Clyde. Condemned to execution the queen prayed for help to St Kentigern, who sent his monks out to fish. The ring was found inside the salmon and her name cleared.

USING THE LAND

While home to a spectacular variety of wildlife, the countryside is home to humans too. It is here that farmers still make their homes and livings, where crops are raised and sheep and cattle grazed. Ancient monuments of many kinds reveal where our ancestors celebrated the passing of both the seasons and their compatriots. These lands offer welcome shelter for climbers and walkers but also bear the scars of conquest, from the remnants of the Roman Antonine Wall to the battlefields where the country's history was shaped. Here, too, unbelievable treasures have been unearthed and art created for all to enjoy.

A ROOF OVER YOUR HEAD
Shelters past and present

Long disappeared, Scotland's earliest homes were basic earth-built dwellings or wattle and daub constructions topped with heather-thatched roofs. Around the Atlantic coast and in the Northern Isles, the remains of circular stone brochs still survive, the oldest some 2,000 years old. These were prestigious dwellings, probably used for both defence and grain storage, but nearly all those visible today date to the 18th century when farming changed dramatically following union with England in 1707. From this time, too, land on large estates was rented out as crofts, small areas of land containing

AMAZING AND EXTRAORDINARY FACTS: THE SCOTTISH COUNTRYSIDE

Many mountaineers have been relieved to find refuge in a bothy, a basic shelter, officially of no more than two stories, left unlocked for anyone to use free of charge. Often ruined cottages that have been somewhat restored, bothies have no electricity or mains water supply, but will often have a wood burning stove and sheepskins for warmth. In these remote havens, tales of ghosts abound.

QUICK FACTS

- Leanach Cottage at the Culloden Battlefield is a typical early 18th century design and a rare survivor.

- The Mountain Bothies Association has a code for bothy use which includes guidance on pollution from human waste.

a dwelling. Simple cottages were called 'butt' and 'ben'. Here the outside door opens into a 'butt', from which another door opens to an inner room or 'ben'. Later the butt came to describe the kitchen end of the cottage, separated by a passage from the parlour or ben. Other common designs were L and T shapes. The red roofs now seen on many cottages, often in scenic locations, dates to corrugated iron being painted with a rust-inhibiting lead paint.

> **EXTRAORDINARY FACT**
>
> At Glencoe is a faithful reconstruction, inspired by archaeological excavations, of a 17th century turf and creel house. It has a turf roof covered with heather and walls of wattle and turf. The cruck frame is of timber and within is a basket like creel, framework woven with wooden branches. Within, animals would have been kept in a byre at one end. There is no fireplace, but smoke drifting through the roof would have warded off invading wildlife. Such cottages were grouped to form small settlements.

FOOD FOR THE NATION
All about oats

They are still a national staple, but it was the Romans who brought oats (*Avena sativa*) to Scotland in the 1st century for horse feed. Even in cool conditions, the crop thrived, thanks to acidic soil, long hours of daylight and plenty of rain. It is slow ripening that gives the best oats their sweet, nutty flavour. By summer, nodding pale green flower heads top bright green foliage. Come mid August, now in gold, they are ready to harvest. While most oats are milled commercially, some ancient mills survive, as at the Blair Atholl, Perthshire, watermill dating to the 1590s. Among cereals, oats are dietary stars. Gluten free, and a proven aid to lowering cholesterol, their high concentration of proteins contains all nine essential amino acids.

Oats

DID YOU KNOW?

Oats are key to many traditional country dishes, from broths to cranachan, a soft fruit brose eaten at harvest home. Oatmeal is graded according to size and use. Quick cooking rolled oats, developed in the USA by the Quaker Oat Company are produced by steaming and rolling pinhead oatmeal.

- Pinhead: Used in haggis and baking oatmeal bread.
- Rough: For porridge, brose and rough oatcakes.
- Medium rough: Butcher's ingredient for mealie puddings.
- Medium and fine: Also for porridge, brose and skirlie (seasoned fried oatmeal with onion and suet).
- Super-fine: For oatcakes and other baking.

EXTRAORDINARY FACT

Dr Samuel Johnson's *Dictionary* of 1755 defined oats as 'a grain which in England is given to horses but in Scotland supports the people'. He later declared that he was making mischief, but was right in many ways. For centuries, farmworkers prepared brose – oatmeal soaked in water then eaten with butter, salt and milk or buttermilk added – for all-day sustenance. Heated in a pot it becomes porridge. Both variations are stirred with a spurtle, a wooden stick prized by a family and always used clockwise and in the right hand for luck. Originally baked in the embers, then griddled, bannocks, made from oats and buttermilk, are traditionally eaten at Beltane, the Gaelic May Day celebration to ensure fortune for crops and animals. At Halloween extra salt was added to create good dreams for the months to come. While bannocks are round and thick, true oatcakes are always thin and triangular.

> **QUICK FACTS**
> - Oat flowers are borne in nodding groups known as panicles.
> - It is said that Atholl brose, flavoured with honey, whisky and often cream, was used by the 1st Earl of Atholl to supress a Highland rebellion in 1475 to spike the rebel leader's well and inebriate his troops.
> - Ancient grains such as the Shetland Black Oat are being revived by some farmers.

THE ESSENTIAL MALT
Among the fields of barley

Without barley there would be no whisky. Nor the staple vital to a Scotch broth or barley bannocks. A field of barley (*Hordeum vulgare*) swaying and shimmering in the breeze is lime green in in spring and a distinctive mid gold by late summer. While ears of wheat stand straight, those of barley, with their long awns (bristly beards), bend over.

- Around 37,500 hectares (92,200 acres) of barley are grown in Scotland each year.
- Where they clasp the stem the leaf bases of barley form smooth, sharp pointed extensions. Those of wheat are short and hairy.
- Wholegrain barley is rich in insoluble fibre which can aid digestion but contains gluten.

EXTRAORDINARY FACT

A resilient ancient grain, possibly the first domesticated grass, barley came to Britain from the eastern Mediterranean between 5,000 and 6,000 years ago. One of the oldest is bere, big or bigg, now mostly cultivated in Orkney and Shetland which can be traced to Neolithic times and is tolerant of poor soils. Known also as '90-day' barley from its short growing season it is the key ingredient of the bere bannock and of malt for beer and whisky. Depending on how the seed is arranged, barley is described as two-row (which is flatter looking) or six-row. Naked barley, which can be four-row, has seeds has no stiff bran-containing casing (hulls) so does not need to be pearled (processed) before they can be eaten.

Frost hardy, slow growing winter barley is sown in November, spring barley in March; both are harvested in August. Most winter barley is used for animal feed and brewing beer and lager; spring barley is ideal for malt distilling.

DID YOU KNOW?

Of all Scotland's barley, 35 per cent is used for whisky. Two-row spring barley's low protein and high starch content makes it ideal for malting, but of the 5,500 known barley strains only 10 are currently approved for Scotch whisky. In malting the grains are first sprouted to release their starch, then dried. The fuel, traditionally peat, used in drying, is key to the final flavour.

Barley

WHAT'S IN THAT FIELD?
Of crops and soil

No haggis dish is complete without neeps and tatties, two key countryside crops. Neeps are named from 'turn-neeps' an early form of turnip introduced from central Europe in the late 18th century, but botanically are swedes, a yellow form of turnip (*Brassica rapa*), which in past times were imported (being sensitive to hard frosts) expensive and enjoyed mainly by the wealthy. A field of swedes is easily identified from the reddish upper parts of the swollen stems sitting above soil level, topped with large green leaves. Potatoes, grown the Andes at least 5,000 years ago were first cultivated near Stirling in 1739 and, although originally greeted with superstition, within two generations had become 80 percent of Highlanders' diets. When in flower, potato fields are a glory of green topped with flowers in shades of white and purple.

> Green manures are becoming ever more visible in the fields, often in bright colour. Fields of red clover, peas and beans whose roots can trap nitrogen from the air make excellent manures. Swathes of pale pinkish purple are the fast-growing scorpion weed (*Phacelia tanacetifolia*), high in nitrogen and highly attractive to bees and other pollinators.

EXTRAORDINARY FACT

Many heritage potatoes are grown in Scotland, helping to preserve a wide gene pool. Among the best are:

• Shetland Black: Kidney shaped with dark purple skins and creamy yellow flesh.

• Arran Victory: Deep purple-blue skin and bright, white flesh. Named to celebrate the end of WWI.

• Highland Burgundy Red: A pink floury flesh that keeps its colour when cooked. Covered with a bright burgundy skin.

• Catriona: Distinctive purple eyes on a smooth skin. Named for Catriona in Robert Louis Stevenson's *Kidnapped*.

• Edzell Blue: A blueish purple named from Edzell in Angus. Excellent blight immunity and bright white flesh.

QUICK FACTS

• Although less severe than Ireland's, Scotland suffered a potato famine from 1846-56 due to blight. From the 1930s to the 1980s school children were granted tattie holidays to help with potato howking or lifting.

• In the southeast swedes are called *baigies*, possibly from the Swedish *rotabagge*, the origin of rutabaga, the vegetable's common name in North America.

Potato plant

THE WONDERS OF WALLS
Enclosing the landscape

Using stones for building, whether for homes or monuments, is a prehistoric skill still on view. As farming evolved, so Scotland's barriers to keep sheep and cattle confined began to emerge, a movement also linked to

Double dyke

EXTRAORDINARY FACT

Reputed to be the highest wall in Scotland the dyke at 1,036 m (3,400 ft), atop Cairn of Claise near Braemar, was begun in the mid 19th century following the sinuous line of the mountains for miles. Extra strength is provided by now rusty iron posts and the wall topped with sharp stones reminiscent of dragons' scales. The men who built it suffered hugely, using hill ponies to carry materials up the mountain in every weather. Additional stones, left by climbers as is the tradition, form a pyramid on the summit wall.

the Highland Clearances of the 18th century. To improve the land, large stones were removed and made into drystane dykes or drystone walls. Erected where the soil

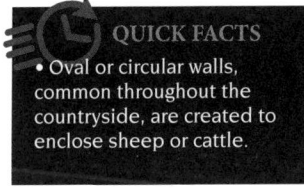

QUICK FACTS
• Oval or circular walls, common throughout the countryside, are created to enclose sheep or cattle.

is too thin for hedges to flourish, they are witness to both geology and history. Many of Scotland's Highland dykes look rough because the hard blocks of quartzite, laid down in the Cambrian era (540 to 485 million years ago), are incredibly hard to cut. At the base, holes or lunkies, which can be easily blocked if necessary, are cut to allow sheep to pass through. Small openings or smoots, less than 20 cm (5 in) high, make easy roaming for rabbits and hares.

Dykes come in many styles. Those of Galloway are an excellent example:
• Single dyke: Large, irregular stones in a single layer. If stones are rounded it is a boulder dyke.
• Double dyke: Small stones with a filling of even smaller stones between the two faces. Topped with larger stones. The most common style in the lowlands.
• Galloway or 'half and half' dyke: Double at the base but with a single layer at the top. Especially common where sheep are kept.

A WOOLLY TALE
Scotland's special sheep

Without its sheep, the kilts, scarves and sweaters synonymous with Scotland would not exist, and although most sheep are kept for meat, some 6,000 tonnes of wool is still gathered annually. Numbering around a 5.43 million, sheep are almost everywhere. But they are not natives, arriving in the Stone Age with Neolithic settlers some 6,000 years ago. Among the oldest breeds still in existence are probably

DID YOU KNOW?

All over the country, but especially in the west and Northern Isles, lambs are increasingly threatened by ravens. In 2023 a farmer in Strathardle, Perthshire, lost 220 lambs to attack by these large corvids which even band together in twos and threes to make their kills.

QUICK FACTS

- Outstanding Scottish cheeses made from ewe's milk include Lanark Blue, Corra Linn and Cairnsmore Ewe.

- Soay sheep can occasionally be seen on the mainland.

- Biddable Hebrideans are widely used for sheepdog training.

- Hebridean lamb is low in fat and cholesterol.

- Early breeds of Cheviots are believed to have been kept by monks.

- A sheep's stomach is the traditional 'container' for a haggis.

the Soay sheep of the eponymous island in the St Kilda group brought by the Norwegians around 500 CE. Small and athletic, with self-shedding fleeces, their coats are shades of brown from chocolate to tan. When Soay was evacuated in 1932, some sheep were taken to Hirta where they remain, although threatened by disease and starvation. Also ancient are the distinctive four (sometimes six) horned small Hebridean sheep. Their wool, subtly shaded in black and brown and absent from face and legs, is two layered and

> ★ AMAZING FACT ★
>
> **ENVIRONMENTAL ACTIVISTS**
>
> Throughout the UK, but especially along Scottish rivers such as the Deveron in the north east, invasive and harmful giant hogweed causes a variety of problems, not least the severe burns on human skin from its toxic sap. Now sheep, which suffer no ill effects from its consumption, are being successfully introduced to rid the river of this menace. In time plants weaken and fail to produce seed heads, each of which can release up to 50,000 seeds a year. Eventually they die.

To protect both lambs and themselves from the weather, from the mid 1800s shepherds of the Borders wore Shepherd's Plaids or Mauds, pieces of woven wool 3 to 4 m (3 to 4 four yards) long and about a metre (1 yard) wide, known as Border Tartans. The usual pattern was crosschecks of black and white, created in the colours of undyed wool.

a superb insulation with a coarse outer layer that is remarkably water resistant. Because they are such efficient browsers, conservationists favour Hebrideans for controlling scrub and preserving biodiversity in grassland, but their predilection for hedgerows means they may need to be confined.

EXTRAORDINARY FACT

Cheviots and Blackfaces, the long tailed sheep most associated with Scotland today, are relative newcomers, introduced largely from the 19th century. Brought from Northumberland, where they were certainly recorded in 1372, Cheviots have white faces and dense, firm cream coloured fleeces still used for making Harris tweed and carpets. Extremely hardy, they can graze the high hills year round without additional feed, except when deep snow makes this impossible. In other breeds, the birth of a black faced sheep is believed to be bad luck unless it is a Blackface, with a striking white coat and large horns. Scotland has two distinct Blackface varieties, the large-framed Perth, usually confined to the northeast, and the medium sized, widespread Lanark with shorter wool. Blackfaces are commonly bred with Bluefaced Leicester rams to produce hardy, fecund Scottish Mules or Greyfaces with high quality meat but very coarse wool.

Blackface sheep

ICON OF THE HILLS
The magnificent Heilan coo

Said to be almost as resilient to cold and wind as arctic dwelling caribou and reindeer, highland cattle, with their majestic, sweeping horns and double coats of shaggy hair – a long, oily outer layer atop a downy undercoat – are countryside icons. It is because the creatures are protected from the cold by their coats, rather than layers of subcutaneous fat, that their meat is remarkably lean, but the attractive red colours now most dominant are not the originals. First of the breed were the black Highland cattle that became commercially important following the Union of 1707 when Scottish beef was critical to the diets of Londoners and to Britain's army and navy. Whatever their colour, which can also be yellow, dun, brindle (subtly striped) or pale silver, Highland cattle live in social groups or folds, named from the open shelters where they were traditionally kept at night. Within the fold are clear orders of dominance, older males holding highest rank but constantly challenged by young adult bulls around two years old.

> **AMAZING FACT**
> **IN BLACK AND WHITE**
> Scotland's famous hornless Belted Galloways whose long black coats are 'broken' by a broad white belt encircling the body are nicknamed Oreo-Cookie Cows in the USA. They are especially tolerant of soft, boggy terrains. Like Highland cattle they have double, weather resistant coats. They are thought to have originated from cross breeding of all-black traditional Galloway cattle with Dutch Lakenvelders.

Highland bull

QUICK FACTS

- Highland cattle can live over 20 years and even breed until they are 18.
- They are excellent mothers; individuals can bear up to 15 calves.
- Queen Elizabeth II began the practice of keeping Highland cattle at Balmoral.
- *The Highland Cattle Herd Book*, published since 1885, lists every pedigree since that date.

EXTRAORDINARY FACT

Highland cattle thrive on poor land with little to forage where they are critical to maintaining upland biodiversity, especially when each individual is paired with four or five sheep. Critical are their grazing, and continual production of dung, plus trampling on invasive species such as bracken, purple moor grass and rhododendrons. They eat lusher species, allowing finer plants a chance to thrive, creating habitats richer in butterflies such as, in Lochaber, the rare chequered skipper and pearl-bordered fritillary.

The droving or moving of cattle formed the basis of Scotland's original road systems. However this could cause controversy between clans and it is said that the Camerons of Lochaber would move their folds by night at Cold Moon, the last full moon of December also known as Locheil's Lantern or the Long Night's Moon.

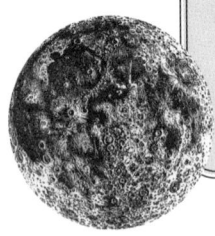

EXTRAORDINARY EQUINES
Horses and their history

Horses of all shapes and sizes are integral to the countryside, but their arrival in Scotland is uncertain. They may have been brought by prehistoric settlers or migrated naturally around 10,000 years ago as the last ice age ended. Certainly they were thriving in the north and east in the 8th century BCE when their images were carved onto stones, depictions remarkably similar to the now rare Eriskay ponies of the eponymous islands in the Outer

Shetland pony

EXTRAORDINARY FACT

FROM THE HIGHLANDS

Descended from crofters' ponies, Highland ponies are Scottish natives with a long history involving horses brought from France and Spain in the 16th century and from England's fells and dales in the 19th. Highland ponies grow thick two-layered winter coats which they shed in spring, revealing smooth coats complementing flowing manes and tails. Now mostly used for riding – including jumping, trekking and carriage driving – they also work on sporting estates to carry deer from the hills and sustenance-containing panniers for participants. Queen Elizabeth II, patron of the Highland Pony Society, kept a stud of working ponies. In many years she named her Balmoral foals according to themes such as birds or islands. A small Highland pony herd with bloodlines dating to 1778 is kept on the isle of Rum where two foals were born in 2023.

Hebrides, once widespread in the western isles and proved to be related to the ancient horses of Iceland and the Faroes. The Eriskay history is as workhorses employed for ploughing and transporting both peat and the seaweed traditionally used as a fertilizer. By the 1970s, only 20 mares and one stallion named Eric remained but, thanks to conservation initiatives, numbers

EXTRAORDINARY FACT

THE POWERFUL CLYDESDALE

In the early 18th century the 6th Duke of Hamilton and John Paterson of Lochlyoch imported Flemish stallions which they mated with the mares of crossbred draught horses (also known as heavy or carthorses) of the Clyde valley to create the Clydesdale breed, a name first recorded in 1826 at an exhibition in Glasgow. Iconic workhorses, with characteristic feathering on their lower legs, Clydesdales were once essential to agriculture and comprised the majority of the 140,000 farm horses in use. Today a few still do farm work but are more likely to be engaged in carriage driving. Most prized are those coloured bay or black with white legs and white facial markings. Within a century of their origin, thousands of Clydesdales were conscripted from Scotland to 'serve' in WWI in which an average of 640 British horses were lost in every week of the conflict. Most famous of the Clydesdales are those used by Budweiser in 1933 to deliver a first case of beer following the end of prohibition. They are now listed as vulnerable by the Rare Breeds Survival Trust.

now exceed 400 across Britain. Mostly with thick, waterproof coats that appear white (technically grey) they are strong and sturdy and widely used in riding programmes for physically and mentally disabled children. Ancient too are Shetland ponies, whose ancestors date to the Bronze Age. Today's domesticated ponies are the result of crosses with horses brought by Norse invaders. Said to be able to survive solely on heather, Shetlands can live outdoors all year. Beyond their work in agriculture they were once employed in mines for hauling coal.

QUICK FACTS

• When the *SS Politician* sank off Eriskay in 1941 the islanders used ponies to haul away the cargo of 250,000 bottles of whisky, an event immortalized in the 1949 film *Whisky Galore!*, remade in 2016.

• A Clydesdale can weigh up to 1,000 kg (157 stone).

• Highland ponies are usually shades of dun – a greyish brown – ranging from near white to 'fox', and 'oatmeal'.

When the Mines Act of 1842 prohibited women and children from working in coal mines, shaggy-coated Shetland ponies with thick manes and tails were quickly substituted. Their strength, sturdiness and intelligence made them ideal for pulling coal carts over rough, uneven ground. Many hundreds were exported from Scotland to the USA for mining work.

RINGS OF STONE
Witness to the ancient world

Once thought to be the remains of wicked men turned to stone for their crimes, or petrified giants who refused to convert to Christianity, the Calanais Stones on the isle of Lewis are Scotland's most famous megaliths. The stones' importance as a celestial calendar and in religious ritual is linked to a lunar phenomenon known as the maximum standstill when, every 18.6 years, the moon appears to dance among the stones like a deity visiting the earth. Set in an extraordinary cross shape, lending credence to their use as a heathen temple, a 13-stone circle averaging 3 m (9 ft) high surrounds a central monolith, its largest sides oriented almost exactly north to south. Radiating outwards are five rows of standing stones, two in a parallel avenue

AMAZING FACT

ON THE LINKS

On the fairway of the second hole of the Lundin Links ladies golf course in Fife (the world's oldest women's golf course) stand three megalithic pillars of sandstone between 4 and 5 m (14 and 17 ft) tall dating to the 2nd millennium BCE. According to legend they mark a site used by Druids in ancient rituals.
A fourth stone was lost in the 18th century.

Both Tomanverie in Aberdeenshire and the Loanhead of Daviot Stone Circle are superb examples of the recumbent stone circles particular to the northeast. Typically consisting of a ring of upright stones with a huge slab laid on its side between two upright stone pillars they were probably used primarily in burial rituals and for tracing the paths of sun and moon.

> **EXTRAORDINARY FACT**
>
> **SPECTACULAR STONES**
> Scotland is rich in other standing stones. On Orkney the majestic ceremonial Neolithic Ring of Brodgar – the 5,000 year old 'dancing giants' – still contains 27 of its estimated original 60 stones, set around a wide earthen trench. Among the carvings on the stones are a cross and the name Bjorn. On the mainland Croft Moraig Stone Circle near Aberfeldy, Perthshire, thought to have begun 5,000 years ago, has 14 wide wooden posts set in a horseshoe shape and surrounded by a ditch. These were later replaced by 8 stones graded in size. Outside the ellipse was a single stone plus a bank of rubble in which were set stones whose position aligned exactly with the midsummer sunrise. Finally, 12 more stones were added in a wide circle. Archaeologists believe that the Tomnaverie Stone Circle in Aberdeenshire began as a series of kerbed cairns in which the dead were buried and where stones were placed around 4,000 years ago. It is thought to have been used by farmers to plot the movement of the sun over the seasons.

out to the north, through which people would funnel towards the centre, the other three leading east, west and south. Within the circle itself, scene of ancient ceremonies and rituals, lies a chambered cairn for burials. Excavations in the 1970s and 80s revealed this to be a later addition but confirmed that the earliest parts of Calanais, erected around 2900 BCE, are as old as those of the Welsh bluestones used to create Stonehenge. The oldest pottery fragments yet found, possibly used in

Calanais Stones

ritual cleansing, date to around 2000 BCE. Within a few miles of the 'main' stones are many other similar monuments on a smaller scale, including Clach an Truseil probably the country's solo standing stone, towering 5.8 m (19 ft) above grass and heather with another 1.8 m (6 ft) below ground. Once part of a ring it would have witnessed the arrival of the Vikings.

KILMARTIN GLEN

The Nether Largie standing stones are among the many highlights of Kilmartin Glen near Oban, Argyll, the mainland's most spectacular collection of Neolithic and Bronze Age remains, containing more than 800 monuments within a 9.6 km (6 mile) radius. Four upright stones (menhirs) are set in pairs about 70 m (76 yards) apart, while seven smaller upright stones, plus one fallen, surround a central menhir. Thought to be astronomically significant, specifically for predicting eclipses, Nether Largie is southeast of the Temple Wood Stone Circle, now comprising 13 of the original 22 stones placed near a timber circle in around 3000 BCE. Later infilled with slabs, this was a burial site, its central area forming a cairn from which grave goods including arrowheads and decorated Beaker pottery have been excavated. The glen contains many other Bronze Age cairns and on its rock faces are a wealth of cup and ring marks – circular hollows surrounded by carved rings, probably linked with religion or magic, or possibly symbolizing a mother goddess's breasts. Within Dunchraigaig Cairn depictions of deer with forked horns were discovered in 2021 and dated to the Neolithic. At Dunadd, an Iron Age fort, it is thought at the Stone of Destiny was first used to crown Scotland's kings.

Beaker pottery

QUICK FACTS

- In 2019 the Calanais Stones 'hosted' a *Call the Midwife* Christmas special.
- In one tale a magic white cow is said to have appeared at the Calanais Stones to save the islanders from starvation.
- A lunar standstill occurred on 21 June 2024.

MESSAGES IN THE STONES
Cairns and their meanings

It is still a custom, as it has been for millennia, to carry a stone from valley to hilltop to add to a cairn on a mountain or moorland. Across barren landscapes cairns can also be way markers, hikers adding more stones as they pass. In Highland folklore it is said that ahead of a battle each solider would place a stone on a pile. Any survivors would remove one, the remainder creating a tribute to the fallen. Cairns can also mark graves or commemorate the dead. At Cairn o'Get, south of Wick in Caithness, a tomb with walls a metre (3 ft) high was erected some 5,000 years ago with massive stone slabs forming lintels above. A pair of upright stones mark the low passageway to the tomb within. At Gallows Hill in Aberdeenshire a Bronze Age cairn became a 17th century place of execution. Criminals climbed the hill to their deaths.

Cairn

EXTRAORDINARY FACT

CLAVA CAIRNS

Four thousand years ago the Bronze Age Clava Cairns, set in the beautiful Balnuaran of Clava, a small wood near Inverness, were almost certainly built to house the dead. Here three surviving cairns lie along raised gravel terrace, oriented northeast to southwest. The northeast cairn is a circular passage grave that would have had a central 4 m (13 ft) domed chamber. Its outer stones (the kerb) were originally coloured red and white and placed in defined sections. Encasing the cairn was a rubble platform, around it a ring of standing stones. By contrast, the central ring cairn has no defined entrance or roof. The stones of inner and outer kerbs have markedly contrasting, textures and heights and are decorated with distinctive shallow cup marks. Archaeologists think that this ring may have been used as a pyre, rather than for burials and, uniquely, paths lead out to the surrounding standing stones. Also set relative the midwinter sun, the southwest cairn has a passage design similar that of the northeast cairn, but taller. Of the sandstone pillars that flank its entrance, one is decorated with cup marks.

QUICK FACTS

- There are at least another 45 similar cairns around the Inverness area.
- Artefacts found at Cairn o' Get include leaf-shaped flint arrowheads, pieces of Neolithic pottery and animal bones.
- Clava Cairns was the inspiration for Craigh Na Dun in *Outlander*.
- Before the Clava Cairns were built the land was used for farming and stones from farm buildings possibly used in their construction.
- The remains of a Medieval chapel have been found near the Clava Cairns.

Clava Cairns

> **DID YOU KNOW?**
>
> The northeast Clava Cairn is placed so that at sunset on the midwinter solstice the sun's rays shines directly into the chamber. When viewed from the northeast the sun would appear to set on the southwest cairn, orientations that may have been critical to burial and cremation rites. Quartz laid on the upper surfaces of the cairns would have shone in dazzling white in both sunlight and moonlight.

THE ROMANS WERE HERE
The story of the Antonine Wall

Their mission to conquer Scotland had failed. In 165 CE the Romans packed their arms and valuables and abandoned the Antonine Wall, their northernmost physical barrier, built on the orders of Emperor Antonius Pius (138-61) to defend themselves against raids from Caledonians wanting to rob their southern neighbours. Many items they were unable to take with them were simply buried. Imperial

AMAZING FACT

ALL IN THE NAME
The Wall is also called Graham's Dyke or Grim's Ditch since legend has it that a warlord named Robert Graham led a Pictish army that successfully broke through the wall near Falkirk. Grim's Ditch links to the legendary Teutonic god Grim, allegedly able to construct huge earthworks overnight. The Wall's remains were also known as the Devil's Dyke.

legacy lives on in the landscape as remnants of the 60 km (37 mile) turf rampart some 3 m (10 ft) high and 4 m (13 ft) wide, built on a stone base and topped with an imposing timber palisade, that ran from Bo'ness on the Firth of Forth to Old Kilpatrick on the Clyde. Along the wall were at least 16 forts housing soldiers, and sometimes their families too, plus smaller fortlets containing bathhouses and latrines. To the north was a massive ditch, 6 m (20 ft) deep and 12 m (40 ft) wide, that could be filled with water if invasion threatened. Beacons were lit at night to warn of imminent attacks. Facing south into the Empire were distance slabs, carved pieces of sandstone set in stone frames, celebrating the achievement of the workforce.

QUICK FACTS

- Building was controlled by the Roman general Quintus Lollius Urbicus.

- Up to 7,000 men were accommodated in the forts.

- A Roman road from the south provided easy access.

- Many coins have been found at the Wall.

- Much of the Wall's archaeology was lost in the building of the Forth and Clyde Canal.

- The Wall is a UNESCO World Heritage Site.

- Many of the artefacts can be seen at the Hunterian Museum in Glasgow and the National Museum of Scotland in Edinburgh.

- Hadrian's Wall, farther south and now completely in England was begun 40 years earlier.

EXTRAORDINARY FACT

Thousands of artefacts left by the Romans who lived and worked at the Wall, even including women and children's leather shoes, paint a vivid picture of daily life. A dice shaker and gaming board reveal their leisure pursuits, while a carving of Hercules symbolizes triumph in battle. Carved stone altars were dedicated to deities; one from Auchendavy fort, inscribed to 'the Spirit of the Land of Britain' is unique. For practicality, soothing, unguent oils for treating wounds were stored in beautiful pots. The Romans made cheese which they pressed in stone containers while circular quern stones were used for grinding grain. At night, forts were illuminated with oil lamps and rooms warmed with underfloor heating, known from the discovery of a box flue tile from a hypocaust system near the commanding officer's house at Mumrills near Falkirk.

Roman shoes

Among the best places to view the remnants of the Antonine Wall in the countryside are:
- Seabags Wood, Bonnybridge south of the Forth and Clyde Canal: A line of ditch and wall running for 400 m (¼ mile) with remaining ramparts.
- Rough Castle, Bonnybridge: One of the best preserved forts with headquarters building, bathhouse, granary and lilia (lily) pits – circular pits in which sharpened stakes were disguised with brushwood.
- Watling Lodge East and West: Tamfourhill Road, Falkirk: Two sections of ditch still near their original dimensions.
- Polmont Woods, Falkirk: Ditch and mound well preserved.

> **DID YOU KNOW?**
>
> In 208 the Emperor Septimius Severus marched north, re-established the Wall, and fought brutal battles with Highland tribes before his death in 211. This explains why it is also known as the Severine Wall.

TREASURE UNEARTHED
The countryside's hidden riches

For detectorists, Scotland is fertile ground and treasure hunting ever more popular. All over the country coins are found almost daily, like those from farmers' fields in Perthshire unearthed in 2024 and dated to the reigns of Antonius Pius (86 -161 CE) and his predecessor the Emperor Hadrian (76-138 CE). To date the largest find of coins is the Dunscore Hoard of more than 8,000, mainly Edward I and II pennies from the 13th and 14th centuries. In 2023 in western Scotland, archaeology student Lucy Ankers discovered during her first dig a pot containing 36 coins under a

AMAZING FACT

GOING FOR GOLD
There are several places in Scotland where you can pan for gold, as in the Lowther Hills around Wanlockhead in Dumfries and Galloway where the sands and gravels in the burns naturally concentrate the precious metal. Gold has been collected here since the early 16th century. Another gold yielding river is the Helmsdale in East Sutherland. Always check ahead – you may need a licence.

stone slab in the fireplace of a house. Since none of the coins date beyond 1680, and the house had connections with Clan MacDonald, it is thought to have been hidden by someone fleeing the Glencoe massacre in 1692. The oldest of the coins date to Elizabeth I.

QUICK FACTS

- The Storr Rock hoard dating from 935 to 940 CE found in 1891 includes coins and treasures from the Baltic and modern day Uzbekistan, so revealing ancient trade routes.

- Treasure was often buried near churches for safe keeping.

- Silver became abundant in the Viking age, coming from Scandinavia and beyond.

- The Galloway vessel is unique in having a surviving lid.

By Scots law, all treasure is owned by the Crown and finds must be reported to the Treasure Trove Unit at the National Museum of Scotland. Here is it assessed and valued and any reward recommended. Rewards are given only to individuals, not to organized teams or their members. Since landowners are not included, it is recommended that as well as seeking permission detectorists make prior written agreements regarding finds to avoid disputes.

EXTRAORDINARY FACT

Buried in around 900 CE, in a time of conflict and uncertainly – doubtless a reason for hiding valuables for safe keeping – the Galloway Hoard was unearthed by a detectorist in 2014 at Balmaghie, Dumfries and Galloway. It is the richest, rarest collection of objects from the Viking era ever found and while its bulk is over 5 kg (11 lb) of silver bullion, it includes treasures from the Anglo-Saxon world, from Ireland and even Asia. The most valuable of these were set inside the Galloway Vessel, a lidded decorated silver gilt pot carefully wrapped in woollen cloth scientifically dated to between 680 and 780 CE. Revealing its Asian origins, the surface bears engravings of leopards, tigers and Zoroastrian symbols. The most valuable item within was the rock crystal jar 'encased' in unique goldwork created using twisted and plaited wire. When examined at the British Museum the gold base was found to bear an inscription that translates as '+ Bishop Hyguald ordered [this] to be made'. Also within was a silver and gold pectoral cross, inlaid with black niello, a paste made from silver and copper sulphide. Superbly created to include images of the Gospel writers Matthew, Mark, Luke and John, it would have been worn on the chest as a symbol of Christian belief. Among the many other objects were brooches and arm rings.

Brooch from the Galloway Hoard

WARRIOR GHOSTS AND LASTING MEMORIALS
The legacy of battle

Their souls are said to haunt Drummossie Moor, along with their restless ghosts. These are the Jacobite dead, numbering around 1,500, slain in less than an hour on 16 April 1746 in the Battle of Culloden, the last major battle on British soil, fought by British government forces led by the Duke of Cumberland against those of Charles Edward Stuart – Bonnie Prince Charlie – claimant to the throne. Now a war grave, where bodies were buried after lying for days on the muddy, windswept moor, there is little heather, believed by some to be a lasting sign of mourning, but the carefully restored terrain is now grazed by goats and Shetland cows, as centuries ago. Skylarks thrive here, despite the belief that no

EXTRAORDINARY FACT

Battlefield historians continue to trace the exact details of Culloden battlefield; the most updated results are marked in a trail marked with flags. Archaeologists continue to find musket and pistol balls, and other ammunition as well as uniform buttons, buckles and cross-bearing pewter amulets that soldiers would have carried for their protection. In 2024 a broken shoe buckle was unearthed, thought to have been worn by Donald Cameron of Lochiel, the hereditary chief of Clan Cameron and a staunch Jacobite, who survived leading the Cameron regiment into battle. Simple standing stone memorials around the site pay tribute to members of individual clans. The 5 m (16 ft) Memorial Cairn, with plaques attached, erected in 1881 by Duncan Forbes, is made of large boulders.

birds sing near the graves, but there are still reported sightings of the Great Scree, a huge, ominous black bird said to have been seen by the Jacobite commander Lord George Murray on the battle's eve. It may also commemorate the 30 wounded Highlanders discovered hiding in the now restored Leanach Cottage on the site and burnt to death. Some visitors still hear the skirl of a lone Jacobite piper and the cries and clashes of hand-to-hand fighting.

VICTORY FOR ROBERT THE BRUCE

He is remembered today with an iconic equestrian statue. In the deep mud of Bannockburn, Robert the Bruce overcame Edward II's English army in 1314. According to legend the English were cruising to victory until an unknown force – the Templars, religious knights with almost super human powers – joined the Scots. A key landmark is the Borestone, a large flat stone with a hole in the centre into which Robert the Bruce is said to have to secured his flagpole on 23 June, the first day of the 48 hour battle. Bruce's victory owed much to the fact that Edward II's troops mustered on the Carse, a plain dominated by peat bog and sticky clay. Meanwhile, Bruce held his troops in the New Park woodland, beyond which many deep ditches had been dug. As the battle ended, the English were unable to retreat across the burn – the 'great ditch' that is now a shallow stream.

Robert the Bruce

QUICK FACTS

- Culloden is 6 km (3.7 miles) east of Inverness.

- A sampler in the Culloden visitor centre, made in 1747 by an 11-year-old girl, depicts a Jacobite being stabbed by a government soldier.

- The centre also displays the May 1746 proclamation issued by the Duke of Cumberland, son of George II, ordering all rebels to surrender their weapons. If armed they could be 'killed on sight'.

DID YOU KNOW?

In 832 CE a battle took place near the village of Athelstaneford, East Lothian between the Picts, under Angus, High King of Alba, and a force of Angles and Saxons led by Althelstan. Dreading defeat, Angus prayed for deliverance. His plea was answered with the appearance of a white saltire (the diagonal cross on which St Andrew had been martyred) in the blue sky above. So, in time, the Saltire became Scotland's flag.

WHERE ART AND NATURE MEET
Sculpture in the landscape

Working with and in nature, creating sculptures from materials which – like ice and snow – may last just a few hours, with twigs and leaves that will decay in time, and with stones and mud, Andy Goldsworthy (b. 1956), creates extraordinary works of art, often using spirals, circles and snaking lines representing his dedication

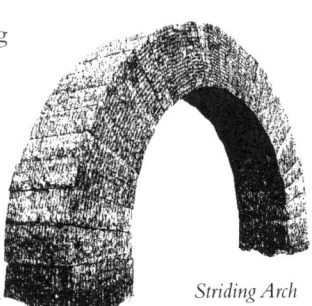

Striding Arch

Millennium Cairn

to the 'energy of making'. Permanent are his Striding Arches, around 4 m (13 ft) high and spanning 7 m (23 ft), each composed of 31 blocks of hand-dressed red sandstone and weighing around 27 tonnes. Three are on hilltops around the natural amphitheatre of Cairnhead in Dumfries and Galloway, sited so that every arch is always be visible from any viewpoint. The fourth curves through a renovated byre (a cowshed) at the glen's heart. Carved on a stone bench alongside are the names of the farming families that once lived there. Other permanent Goldsworthy works include Millennium Cairn, built in 2000 near Penpont close to his home.

EXTRAORDINARY FACT

THE CRAWICK MULTIVERSE

In 2005 the Duke of Buccleuch invited artist and cultural theorist Charles Jencks (1939-2019) to design an inspiring landscape in a former open cast coal mine near Sanquhar in Dumfries and Galloway. From this 'dull ground' covering 22 hectares (55 acres) emerged his sculptural panorama encompassing four natural environments: grassland, mountains, water and desert. Even the slag from the mining process was used. A network of paths and landforms now represents black holes, galaxies and the sun within themes of astronomy, cosmology and space exploration.

DID YOU KNOW?

As well as his famous Kelpies sculptor Andy Scott (b.1964) has created around Alloa a series of galvanized steel and bronze sculptures, each composed of thousands of small metal sections. Outside the town, *River Spirit*, a 6 m (19½ ft) female figure, faces the Forth; she holds in her foliage hands a ribbon-like profile of the river. Nearby is *Stride*, or *Air Spirit*, a 4 m (13 ft) male figure heading towards the Ochil Hills and representing the countryside's rich biodiversity.

QUICK FACTS

- The poignant carved wooden sculptures of the Remembrance Woodland in South Ayrshire, commemorating the fallen of WWI, are made of Norway spruce felled specifically for the project and based on contemporary photographs.

- The Mormond Hill Stag, made from thousands of boulders of white quartz in the Aberdeen countryside in 1870 re-emerged in 2023 thanks to the work of volunteers.

- Made of 81 rocks and constructed in 1995 the Touchstone Maze above Strathpeffer follows ancient patterns that integrate geology and astronomy.

INDEX

Adomnan, St 95
Affric, Glen 48, 54
Affric, Loch 91
airglow 13
Aldons Quarry 25
ale, heather 66
Alloa sculptures 135
alpine cinquefoils 81
alpine flora 79-81
alpine gentians 79
amethyst deceiver 43, 96
Angus, King 133
Ankers, Lucy 128-9
antlers 22, 23, 57, 58
Antonine Wall 125-8
Arctic bearberries 60
Ardchattan Priory 78
Argyll rainforest 8, 49
Arran, isle of 24
Atholl brose 106
auroras 13-15
avalanches 16
Awe Loch 90, 91
azure hawkers 48

Ballantine, Georgina 100
Bannockburn 78, 132
barley 106-7
bats 46-8

Beag, Loch 82
bearberries 61
Bearsden Shark 25
Beast of Bennachie 72
beavers 87-9, 93
beefsteak fungus 44
Beira 77
bell heather 66
Beltane 105
Belted Galloways 115
Ben Nevis *see* Nevis, Ben
bere 107
Bicellum brasieri 24
big cats 71, 72
Big Grey Man 12
bilberries 60-1
Black Cuillin 27
black darters 48
black grouse 34, 40-1, 76
blackberries 61
Blackface sheep 114
blackthorn 77
bladderworts 90
blaeberries 60-1
Blair Atholl 104
blanket bogs 75-6, 89
'blue powder' days 15
bodach 97, 98
bog asphodel 80

bogbean 90
Bone Caves 26
Border Tartans 113
bothies 103
bracken 62-3
Braeriach 15
brochs 102
Brocken Spectre 12
Brodgar Neolithic Ring 121
Brora 16
Brown, John 70
brown long-eared bats 46
Bruar Falls 81-2
Burns, Robert 81-2, 84
butt and ben 103
butterflies 46-9, 50, 116
butterworts 73

Cailleach 29
Cairn o'Get 123, 124
Cairngorms 12, 15-16, 22, 26, 88, 89, 98
cairns 123-5
Calanais Stones 120-2, 123
Caledonian Forest 32-4, 40

Cameron, Clan 131
Camerons of Lochaber 116
caoineag 82, 98
capercaillie 34, 39, 40-1
Carmichael, Alexander 97
castoreum 89
cat-sìth 71
cattle 63, 115-16
cauliflower fungi 44
ceps 44, 96
Cernunnos 57
chanterelles 44
Charlie, Bonnie Prince 17, 131
cheese 112
chequered skippers 47, 48, 50, 116
Cheviot sheep 112, 114
chicken of the woods 43, 96
Chisholm, Clan 63
Ciste Mhearad 16
Clach an Truseil 122
Claise Cairn 110
Clava Cairns 124-5
clouds 11; inversion 10
clubmosses 63
Clydesdale horses 85, 118, 119
Columba, St 95

common heath moths 68
common scoters 76
Conan House 84
Corbett, John Rooke 28
Corbetts 28
cotton grass 74, 76
Cova, Glen 54
cowberries 61
cranberries 60, 61
crane flies 76
Crawick Multiverse 134
Croft Moraig Stone Circle 121
crofts 102-3
Cromdale hills 22
cross-leaved heath 66
crossbills 26, 34
crowberries 60
Cuillin ranges 29
Culloden, Battle of 17, 67, 92, 103, 131-2, 133
Cumberland, Duke of 131, 133

Dalmellington Tip 25
damselflies 48
dead man's fingers 43
deer 57-9
Den Finella Waterfall 83
Derry, Glen 54
devil's tooth fungus 43

dingy skippers 47
Dochart Falls 83
dock 93
Donald, Clan 101
Donald, Percy 28
Donalds 28
Doon Hill 33
Douglas, David 35
Douglas fir 35
downy birch 96
downy willows 80
dragonflies 48
drooping saxifrage 55
Druids 120
Duich, Loch 99
Dunadd Iron Age fort 122
Dunchraigaig Cairn 122
Dunscore Hoard 128
dykes 111

eagles 30-2
Eas a' Chual Aluinn 82
edible fungi 44
Edward II, King 132
Eilean Donan 99
elders 77
Elizabeth II, Queen 116, 117
emperor moths 68
Eriskay ponies 117-19
Essex skippers 47

Etive Glen 54
European larch 35
Ewan of Cluny 67
Exidiopis effusa 16

fairies 15, 33, 57, 62, 67, 78, 92, 96, 98
Fairy Pools 96
fallow deer 59
Famous Grouse whisky 70
featherworts 51
Fergus, Loch 89
ferns 49, 51, 53, 62-4
ferox trout 94
filmy ferns 64
Findhorn Valley 31
fir clubmoss 63
Five Sisters of Kintail 27
Fleming, Ian 54
Flow Country 8, 75-6
Forbes, Duncan 131
forget-me-nots 79
Fortingall Yew 78
fossils 8, 24-5, 82
foxfire fungi 45
freedom to roam 9
fungi 42-3, 96

Galloway Hoard 129, 130
Gallows Hill 123
Garten, Loch 48, 86, 87, 98
Garve, Loch 85
Glen Coe 55, 104
Glencorse 55
Glenmard Wood 25
glens 53-7, *see also individual glens*
Gloag, Matthew 70
Gloag, Philippa 70
Glorious Twelfth 68
glue crust fungus 42
gold panning 128
golden eagles 30-2
Goldsworthy, Andy 133-4
Graham, Robert 125
Grampians 29, 32
graptolites 24
Gray, Hugh 95
great diving beetles 76
Great Glen 8, 53, 93, 95
Great Scree 132
green elf cup 43, 45
Green Loch 92
green manure 108
Grey Mare's Tail 82, 91
Grim 125
grouse *see* black grouse; red grouse

Hadrian's Wall 126

haggis 108, 112
Hamilton, Duke of 118
hares 20-1
Harris, isle of 31
hart's tongue ferns 64
hawthorn 77-8
hazel gloves fungus 42
heather 65-8
Hebridean sheep 112, 113, 114
hedgehog mushrooms 44, 96
Helix Park 85
Helmsdale river 128
hen of the woods 43
Highland cattle 115-16
Highland Clearances 8-9, 36, 111
Highland ponies 117, 119
hogweed 113
honey 66, 67
horses 63, 83-4, 85, 117-19
horsetails 63
Hutton, James 55

ice pancakes 16
ichthyosaurs 24
Ida 60

James I, King 87

Jencks, Charles 134
Johnson, Dr Samuel 105
junipers 79

Katrine, Loch 91
Kellas cats 71
kelpies 83-5
Kentigern, St 101
Kerrera 24
Killarney ferns 64
Kilmartin Glen 122
Kirk, Revd Robert 33
Knapdale 87

Lady Burn 25
Landseer, Sir Edwin 58
Languoreth, Queen 101
large heath butterflies 49
Lawers, Ben 79-81
Leanach Cottage 103, 132
lekking 40-1
Lewis, isle of 120
Lewisian Gneiss 26
lichens 22, 49, 50, 52-3
Lindgren, Dr Ethel 22
ling 65-6, 67
liverworts 51, 81
Loanhead of Daviot Stone Circle 120
lochs 89-98, *see also individual lochs*

lodgepole pine 35
Lomond, Ben 27
Lomond, Loch 31, 87, 90, 92-3
lone oak 90
lover's knot moths 68
Lowther Hills 128
Loyne, Glen 33
lunar standstill 120, 123
Lundin Links 120
Lurchers Crag 12
Lyon, Glen 54

MacDonald, Clan 129
McDonell, Donald 97
Macdui, Ben 12, 27, 29
MacGregor, Clan 34
Macgregor, Rob Roy 91
Mackay, John 95
MacLeod, Clan 96
MacPherson, Clan 67
McSorley, Gerald 94
Mallachie, Loch 97, 98
Malvina 67
Marilyns 28
Measach Falls 83
Meavaig, Glen 56
metal detectors 128-30
midges 17-19, 50
mining 119
Mirrie Dancers 13
moonworts 63, 64

Morag 96-7
Morar, Loch 90, 91
Morlich, Loch 89, 98
Mormond Hill Stag 135
mosses 49, 50, 51, 73, 74, 76, 81
moth caterpillars 68
mountain avens 81
mountain bladder ferns 64
mountain hares 20-1
Muick, Loch 91
muirburn 65
Muirward Wood 34
Mull, isle of 31
Munro, Sir Hugh 28
Munros 27, 28
Murray, Lord George 132
Murray, Sarah 16

neeps 108
Ness, Loch 31, 90, 93-6, 99
Nessie 95, 97, 99
net-leaved willows 80
Nether Largie standing stones 122
Nevis, Ben 29, 54
Nevis, Glen 54
Newman's lady ferns 81
Njuggles 84

noble fir 35
noctule bats 47
Nordmann fir 35
northern damselflies 48
northern emeralds 48
Norway spruce 34, 35

oak eggar moths 68
oak polypore 45
oats 104-6
Oich, Loch 97
orange peel fungus 43
Orkneys 30, 107, 121
ospreys 86-7
otters 98-9
oyster mushrooms 45

Paterson, John 118
pearl bordered fritillary 50, 116
pearl mussels 88
peat 8, 73-6, 107
penny buns 44
Pentland Hills 25
pine martens 38-9, 41
Pitlochry 101
Pityoulish Loch 84
Pliny the Elder 32
Plodda Falls 83
Plutonism 55
pollution 90
Polmont Woods 127

potatoes 108-9
ptarmigans 20-1
pterosaurs 24
purple hairstreak butterflies 46-7

rainfall 10
rainforest 8, 49-53, 59, 64
Ranald, Clan 67
raspberries 60, 61
ravens 112
red deer 57-9
red grouse 68-70, 76
red squirrels 34, 36-7, 39, 53
Reelig, Glen 35
reindeer 22-3
Remembrance Woodland 135
Rhydderch, King 101
Rhymer, Thomas 78
Richards, A J 97
Rines, Robert 94
Robert the Bruce 78, 132
rock lady's mantles 81
rock ptarmigans 20-1
roe deer 59
Romans 125-8
rookooking 40
Rough Castle 127

rowans 77, 78
Rum, isle of 31

salmon 100-1
Saltire 133
Samhain 71
scorpion weed 108
Scotch argus 47
Scots pine 32-4
Scott, Andy 85, 135
Scott, Peter 94
Scott, Sir Walter 54, 91
sculpture 133-5
Seabags Wood 127
selkies 96
Septimius Severus, Emperor 128
Shakespeare, William 78
sheep 110, 111, 112-14
Shetland ponies 119
Shine, Adrian 95
shooting 68-9
Sibbald, Sir Robert 20
sika deer 59
Silberschlag, Johann 12
Simpson, William 97
Sitka spruce 35
Skeen, Loch 82, 91
skipper butterflies 47
Skye, Isle of 24, 31, 56, 63, 82, 96
Sligachan, Glen 56

sloes 77
snow 15-17, 20
snow bunting 21
Soay sheep 112, 113
Spectre of the Bloody Hand 98
sphagnum moss 73, 74, 76
'Sphinx' 15-16
spiders 74
spindrift 16
standing stones 120-3, 131
Steall Falls 54
Steve 15
Stevenson, Robert Louis 66
stoats 20-1
stone circles 120-3
Stone of Destiny 122
stone walls 110-11
Stormont, Loch 89
Storr Lochs Monster 24
Storr Rock hoard 129
Striding Arches 134
Suilven 27
sun-jumping spiders 74
swedes 108, 109

Tay, Loch 91
Templars 132
Temple Wood Stone Circle 122
Three Sisters 27
Thrim 17
Tilt, Glen 53, 55
Tomnaverie Stone Circle 120, 121
Torridon, Loch 24
Touchstone Maze 135
trailing azaleas 81
trilobites 24
trout 94
turf and creel house 104
turnips 108
twinflower 34

Utsi, Mikel 22

vendace 82
Victoria, Queen 29, 67

Wailing Widow Falls 82
wallabies 93
water voles 88, 90
waterfalls 81-3
Waterson, George 87
Watling Lodge 127
waxcaps 42
weather 10-12
Wetherall, Marmaduke 94
whiskered bats 46
whisky 58, 70, 79, 106-7, 119
white-faced darters 48
white-tailed eagles 30-1
wildcats 34, 71-2
willows 80
Wilson, William 51
Wilson's filmy ferns 64
wind 11
woodlands 32-6, 49-53
woolly willows 80

yellow water lilies 90
yews 78

OTHER TITLES IN OUR AMAZING AND EXTRAORDINARY FACTS SERIES

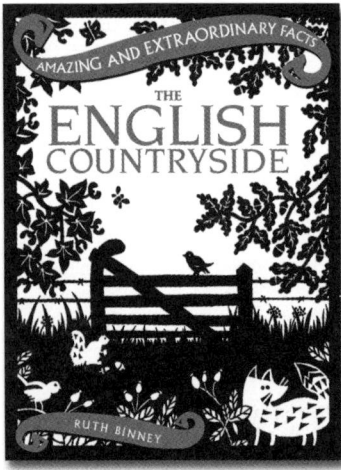

Amazing and Extraordinary Facts:
The English Countryside
Ruth Binney
ISBN: 978-1-910821-45-9

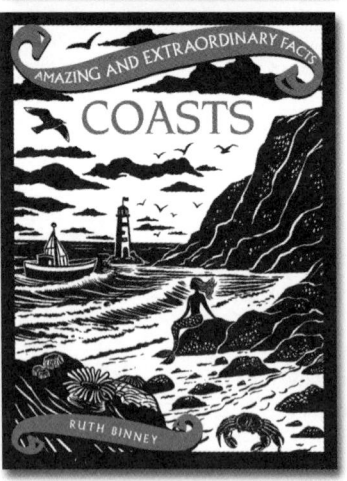

Amazing and Extraordinary Facts:
Coasts
Ruth Binney
ISBN: 978-1-910821-39-8

Amazing and Extraordinary Facts:
Scotland
Douglas Skelton
ISBN: 978-1-910821-14-5

Amazing and Extraordinary Facts:
Ireland
Sarah Elliott
ISBN: 978-1-910821-13-8

For more great books visit our website at **www.rydonpublishing.co.uk**

THE AUTHOR

Ruth Binney has been studying the natural world for most of her life. She holds a degree in Natural Sciences from Cambridge University and has been involved in countless publications during her career as an editor. She is the author of many successful natural history, gardening and nostalgia titles, including *Flower Garden Secrets*, *Plant Lore and Legend* plus *The English Countryside and Coasts* from Rydon Publishing's bestselling Amazing and Extraordinary Facts series. A frequent visitor to Scotland since childhood, she lives in Cardiff. www.ruthbinney.com